RSNC Guide to
British
Wild
Flowers

RSNC Guide to
British Wild Flowers

Franklyn Perring

Illustrated by Roger Gorringe

Country Life Books

Contents

Published by Country Life Books,
an imprint of Newnes Books,
a Division of The Hamlyn Publishing Group Limited,
84-88 The Centre, Feltham, Middlesex, England,
and distributed for them by
The Hamlyn Publishing Group Limited,
Rushden, Northants, England.

Second impression 1985
ISBN 0 600 35617 5
Printed in Spain

Introduction

This book has been written for beginners — those who would like to know the names of the wild flowers they see on a country walk or even when waiting for a bus into town but are daunted by the sheer numbers involved. Over 1700 plants are native or have become naturalised in the British Isles: whereas the budding bird watcher, for example, has a much easier task with only about 220 resident breeding birds or regular winter visitors and migrants to tackle.

This is *not* a comprehensive guide to the identification and naming of all those 1700 — there are plenty of excellent reference works of that kind and they are listed on page 125. Rather it is a 'go-between' for those who think they know nothing, want to know more, but don't know where to start. If you use this book in the way I suggest you could soon recognise and put a name to 330 of our most familiar wild flowers and that would include the vast majority of those you are likely to see when out and about in the countryside near your home.

You may think that recognising and giving names to even 330 plants is a feat beyond your powers but you would be wrong. Human beings, even little children, are able to recognise and name hundreds of relatives and friends, especially if they see them often and are properly introduced. This book aims to introduce you to a few new friends and their relatives at a time, helping you to get to know them by their odd or unique characteristics — and wherever possible an old friend is used to make the introductions.

Come into the garden

Nearly everyone who steps through the French windows on to a lawn surrounded by flower beds will find him or herself amongst old botanical friends. Any list made of those you recognise in the herbaceous border would surely include poppies, pansies, forget-me-nots, foxgloves, antirrhinums, scabious, teasels, bluebells and heathers, whilst a stroll past the rockery and the herb garden to the vegetable patch might well add stonecrops, rockroses, thyme, mint, marjoram, parsley, parsnips, strawberries, carrots and cabbages. And we all recognise dandelions, docks, nettles and thistles wherever they grow.

Garden flowers and vegetables all have their origins in the wild. Many of these 'originals', like primroses, forget-me-nots and bluebells, are such attractive flowers that we continue to cultivate the wild form: others, like rockroses and pansies, have been 'improved' by selection and breeding to produce forms with more showy flowers which, however, still retain the essential characteristics of their wild parents. Wild flowers from abroad, especially from southern Europe, have long been cultivated. Many have escaped from gardens and behave like wildflowers — several of these are therefore familiar to gardeners, for example red valerian, feverfew, monkeyflower and evening primroses.

This familiarity with garden plants and their names is used to lead the reader from the known to the unknown. The core of the book is a series of 56 two-page spreads with text and pictures relating to each other. Wherever possible, the title of the spread uses English names of garden plants or weeds, for example poppies, daisies, clovers and mints. The best way to use the book is to select one of these groups for study and then take the book into the garden at the flowering season indicated. In most cases the descriptions start with reference to the relevant garden plants and give an idea where they are most likely found, whether it be the lawn, the paths, walls, flower beds, potato patch or shrubbery. First identify the plant from its picture and then read the text on the facing page, checking that the features describe the plant you have in front of you. If you come across an unfamiliar term in the plant descriptions, look it up in the glossary on pages 122-4.

It is important to *take the book to the plants*. If you pick just a flower and a few upper leaves, you may well be ignoring the most useful identification feature: in many cases it is the shape of the whole plant, including the arrangement of the branches, the texture of the leaves at ground level or the colour of the base of the stem, which provide the solution. If you have no garden or only a very small one, then visit the nearest park or take the book with you when you go to stay with friends in the country.

Once you have learnt to recognise and name wild flowers in the garden, you are ready to take to the wider countryside. To start with look particularly for species which are similar to those you know already but are somehow different — the 'look-alikes'. For instance, in the garden you may have found greater plantain (page 88) growing on a heavily trodden path, but in a nearby old meadow, especially in lime-rich areas and even in some old lawns, you may come across another rosette of broad leaves which, because they are covered in white hairs, belong to hoary plantain. This is a straightforward example of a common garden weed which has a less common relative in the wild and there are others like fat-hen (page 30) and red goosefoot, or lesser trefoil (page 36) and hop trefoil. However, in some cases one or two 'garden' plants have a whole range of 'look-alikes' which could present problems. In these cases, notably parsleys (pages 48-53) and forget-me-nots (page 68), a special, simplified chart has been prepared which explains which parts of the plant to study to arrive at a definite identification. Comprehensive instructions on using these charts are given in the appropriate place.

The arrangement of the pages

In nearly every case the plants on a double-page spread belong to a single *family* of wild flowers. Occasionally, as in pansies and violets (page 20) or speedwells (pages 74-7) to a single *genus*.

A genus is a group of related species or individual plants which tend to look alike but which differ in a number of characteristics which are constant and by which they may be recognised. All genera (plural of genus) have the same initial scientific name; thus pansies and violets belong to the genus *Viola* and speedwells to the genus *Veronica*.

A family is a group of related genera which do not necessarily look alike superficially but have features in common, especially of flower structure and seed and fruit formation, which indicate a common ancestry. An obvious example is the family Compositae (pages 98-107): all the genera and species in it have heads of many individual flowers (florets) but otherwise the members of this family exhibit a very wide range of forms.

In most books on plant identification (Floras) the species are arranged in a sequence of families which bears some relationship to the evolution of flowering plants from the most primitive to the most advanced forms. To help readers themselves evolve to more comprehensive works such a sequence is followed here, from pages 10 to 115. However, on pages 108-9 and 116-21 the species are not grouped according to family but to another common feature. Pages 108-9 are of plants from five families all having spikes of yellow flowers: pages 116-19 are common flowers of wetlands and pond margins, whereas pages 120-21 includes common species of woodland and shrubbery not dealt with elsewhere.

Looking at wild flowers and remembering them

Throughout the book reference is made to particular features of the plants, many of them small and difficult to see with the naked eye. No budding botanist can properly manage without a hand-lens. A simple one which gives a magnification of ×10 and folds away into a protective aluminium case is perfectly adequate. This will enable you to see glandular or star-shaped hairs, or the minute teeth on the margin of a leaf. A tip about using a lens — put it to your eye and *bring the plant to the lens*, not the other way about.

Though this book will help you to recognise 330 of the commonest wild flowers, you still have the task of remembering their names. One of the easiest ways is to make a collection of dried specimens — a *hortus siccus* or 'dried garden' — of all the wild flowers you find and identify in and around the garden, labelling them boldly and clearly. In preparing and then perhaps mounting your specimens it is necessary to handle them several times: this discipline is very effective in making the names stick.

To make a good dried specimen you will need a plant press, but all the materials required are at hand. They are:

> 2 wire cake racks (about 30×45cm)
> old newspapers
> corrugated cardboard
> jeweller's tags
> nylon string (binder twine if available)

Tear newspapers into rectangles twice the size of the cake racks and cut two or three pieces of corrugated cardboard to the same size as the cake rack with the corrugations running across the shorter dimension, *not* lengthways. Collect specimens which include as much of a plant as possible, or at least illustrate its main features, e.g. any underground stems or bulbs, basal leaves, stem leaves, flowers and seeds or fruits.

Positioning one of the cake racks legs downwards, place a piece of newspaper on it, allowing only half the paper to rest on the rack. Arrange the plant on that half of the newspaper, tie a jeweller's tag to the plant with the name clearly written on it, and then fold the other half of the paper over the plant. Repeat this routine for about ten specimens before inserting one of the pieces of corrugated cardboard; then prepare another ten and so on. Thirty specimens are enough for any one pressing. Add the other cake rack (legs upwards) and tie the whole 'parcel' with the string no tighter than you would a normal parcel. The object is not to press the moisture out of the specimens but to dry them under gentle pressure.

Now place your parcel in a warm, dry place (the airing cupboard is ideal or on a shelf above a radiator), resting it on one of its long sides so that the holes of the corrugations are vertical and warm air can pass through, drying the paper which has absorbed moisture from your plants. By this means thin-leaved specimens and those which are already dry-looking (e.g. grasses) can be taken out after 24 hours. Other thicker-leaved plants (especially stonecrops) take longer and it will help if the newspaper is changed every day or so. The used paper can quickly be dried on the radiator ready for the next change.

If you want to make a permanent collection then the dried plants can be mounted on white paper, using thin strips of glued paper to hold the plant down. Sellotape is only satisfactory for temporary collections. If you have used cake-trays about 30 × 45cm, then A4 paper will be an ideal size. Label each sheet with the English and scientific names and include a description of where it grew, the place and the date.

The modern alternative to a *hortus siccus* is a camera. A standard single-lens reflex and a single extension tube is all the equipment needed to produce slides or prints of the whole plant or parts showing identification features. Here again, taking photographs, writing the name in a notebook, mounting the prints or labelling the slides all help to imprint the names on the memory.

Whichever method you choose, a first objective in using this book might be to build up a collection of all the wild flowers found in your garden. It would not be unusual if you found more than a hundred species over a two- or three-year period.

In addition it is now possible to get to know more wild flowers by raising them yourself from seed. Several firms specialise in wild flowers of native British origin. The four following are particularly recommended:

John Chambers,
15 Westleigh Road,
Barton Seagrave,
Kettering,
Northants NN15 5AJ

D. MacIntyre, BSC, MSc,
Emorsgate Seeds,
Emorsgate,
Terrington St. Clement,
King's Lynn, Norfolk PE34 4NY

W. W. Johnson & Son Ltd.,
Boston,
Lincolnshire,
PE21 8AD

Suffolk Herbs,
Sawyers Farm,
Little Cornard,
Sudbury,
Suffolk.

However, if you do raise them successfully please do *not* introduce them into the countryside. Such action would not only be biologically undesirable, but also usually would be completely ineffective because of the very specialised requirements of species in the wild.

Wild plants and the law

One of the advantages of collecting in your own garden is that here you can dig up plants without breaking the law. It is illegal for anyone, without permission of the owner or occupier, to uproot any wild plant. So elsewhere, unless you specifically ask, you may only pick wild flowers, not uproot them. As a general rule even then, only pick flowers when they are common or plentiful in the locality. If you limit your collecting to those covered by this book you will certainly not be in danger of picking any of the sixty-two very rare plants which are totally protected. Details of the law governing wild plants are obtainable from the Royal Society for Nature Conservation, The Green, Nettleham, Lincoln LN2 2NR, which also sells posters illustrating these sixty-two protected plants.

Buttercups and their relations

Buttercups belong to a large family, Ranunculaceae, which includes many well-known garden flowers such as aconites, anemones, aquilegias, clematis, delphiniums and hellebores. Gardens will have a few wild members.

The commonest buttercup is creeping buttercup **E** which spreads by runners which root at frequent intervals. It can form large patches on lawns or in grass paths, from which it may spread to become an annoying weed. Distinguished gardens with old lawns may have the much less vigorous bulbous buttercup **D**, recognised by the bulbous base to its stem just below ground level. In a verge or grassy field, is meadow buttercup **C**, the only one of the three in which the terminal lobe of the 3-lobed leaf lacks a stalk.

Buttercups were so named because wherever cows grazed the pastures became full of buttercups (which are unpalatable and poisonous) and it was natural to link the yellow flowers with the colour of butter. Cows treading around the margin of a pond make an ideal habitat for celery-leaved buttercup **F**, instantly recognised by its glossy, dark green, kidney-shaped leaves, often lying flat on the muddy surface. The small wet corner may harbour two more 'buttercups': lesser spearwort **G** has buttercup-like flowers but the leaves are all long, narrow and unlobed, though sometimes toothed; marsh-marigold **H** has large kidney-shaped leaves and carries flowers with a variable number of golden yellow, petal-like sepals (up to 8) and no true petals.

Lesser celandine **B** has leaves which, though smaller, are a similar shape to marsh-marigold and it has the same variability in the number of 'petals' — there may be as many as 12, above 3 green sepals. Two forms are widespread in Britain: the one found in garden shrubberies, forming golden carpets in spring, develops bulbils at the base of its leaves by May, whereas the wild form found in woods and meadows normally lacks them. Wood anemone **A** is also often grown in garden shrubberies. There is only one kind of 'petal', which varies in number from 5 to 9 and in colour from white through pink to reddish purple.

A Wood anemone *Anemone nemorosa.* Flowers open in bright sunshine but in dull weather or at night close and droop their heads. Flowers March—May.

B Lesser celandine *Ranunculus ficaria.* Also called 'pilewort' from the shape of its underground root tubers and because it was supposed to cure piles. Flowers March—May.

C Meadow buttercup *Ranunculus acris.* Stalks beneath flowers smooth, not ribbed, and sepals upright, encircling the petals. Flowers May—July.

D Bulbous buttercup *Ranunculus bulbosus.* Stalks beneath flowers ribbed and sepals reflexed, encircling the stalk. Flowers May—June.

E Creeping buttercup *Ranunculus repens.* Stalks beneath flowers ribbed but sepals upright, encircling the petals. Flowers May—August.

F Celery-leaved buttercup *Ranunculus sceleratus.* The English name is falsely derived from *sceleratus*, Latin for wicked or vicious, referring to its poisonous properties. Flowers May—September.

G Lesser spearwort *Ranunculus flammula.* The Latin name *flammula* means a little flame, referring to the burning taste of the poisonous leaves. Flowers May—September.

H Marsh-marigold *Caltha palustris.* Also called kingcup, which is derived from Anglo-Saxon *copp*, head: unopened flowers resemble gold studs worn by kings. Flowers March—July.

Poppies

Poppies are amongst the most brilliant wild flowers, decorating railway banks, road verges and waste places with a blaze of scarlet from June to August. Since the use of weed-killers, cornfields covered in poppies are no longer a common sight but, on recently disturbed ground, they may occur in thousands as they did in Flanders in the wake of battle during the First World War. Poppy Day is a reminder of the red blood spilt on the soil from which this flower grew.

The common poppy **A** has smooth, globular capsules but four other, slightly different species may be found in similar places. Rough poppy **B** also has round capsules but they are covered in long clasping hairs. Likewise prickly poppy **C** has hairy capsules but they are twice as long as wide. Two other poppies with long capsules occur but in both they are hairless. Long-headed poppy **D** which, when the flowering stalk is broken, exudes a white juice, and yellow-juiced poppy *Papaver lecoqii*, a rare species of calcareous soils in south and east England (not illustrated).

The milky latex which exudes from the scarified, immature capsules of opium poppy **E** is the source of the drug opium, for which the plant is cultivated in the Far East. In Britain the capsules were used as a source of 'syrup of poppies', said to have been a favourite remedy for children when a sedative was required! It escaped from cultivation and is still a frequent annual weed. It is easily distinguished by its scarcely divided leaves and white or pale lilac flowers.

Greater celandine **F**, with four petals like other members of the poppy family, was also introduced to Britain for its medicinal properties. The poisonous latex it produces when the skin is broken is bright orange and was formerly used as a cure for warts; it was also believed that the juice cured sore eyes by removing cloudy spots on the eyeball (neither remedy can be recommended). This plant never escapes far from the garden, often only to the base of the nearest brick wall.

A Common poppy *Papaver rhoeas*. Round, smooth capsules; petals bright scarlet, unspotted; hairs on flowering stalks spread at right angles. Flowers June—August.

B Rough poppy *Papaver hybridum*. Round capsules covered in clasping hairs; petals crimson with purplish-black blotch at base; rare cornfield weed in south east of England. Flowers June—July.

C Prickly poppy *Papaver argemone*. Long capsules with few spreading hairs; petals pale scarlet with dark blotch at base. Flowers June—July.

D Long-headed poppy *Papaver dubium*. Long, smooth capsules; petals scarlet, unspotted; hairs on flowering stalks clasping; latex white. Flowers June—July.

E Opium poppy *Papaver somniferum*. Lobed, dusty-green leaves clasp the stem at their base; petals white or pale lilac. Flowers July—August.

F Greater celandine *Chelidonium majus*. Perennial with long, slender capsules; brittle stems break to exude bright orange latex. Flowers May—August.

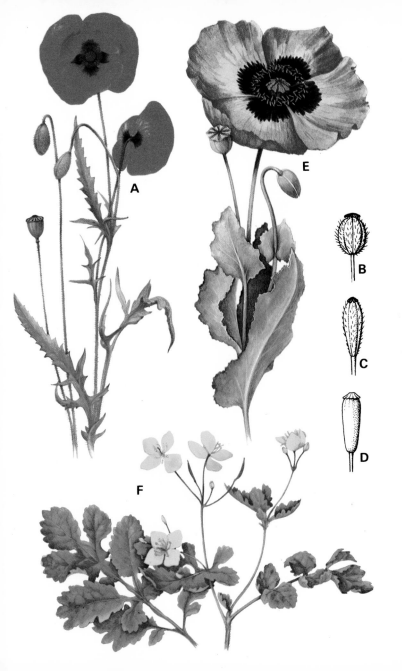

A

E

B

C

D

F

'Cabbages': yellow flowered

When spring comes, suddenly cabbages and kale, sprouts and sprouting turn the kitchen garden yellow. Each flower has four separate sepals and petals arranged in a cross-shape, from which the family name, the Cruciferae, is derived.

When these bolted cabbages have been cleared, another yellow crucifer may appear as a weed, charlock **D**. The leaves are more like turnip's than the bluish-green of cabbage and were boiled and eaten as a vegetable in the Hebrides.

Rape **C** is closely related to the turnip but has flower buds which overtop the open flowers whereas in turnip the open flowers overtop the buds. Rape is increasingly grown as a crop for the oil from its seeds, sowing bright golden squares into the landscape patchwork in springtime.

Another garden crop which has a wild relative is radish. The cultivated radish has a swollen tap-root which we eat, and seed pods which are not markedly constricted between the seeds. Wild radish **E**, which may occur in garden beds, and is frequent as an arable weed, especially on acid soils, has no swollen tap-root but the pods are constricted between the seeds.

Just beyond the garden in farmyard, hedge or between the paving stones in town the wiry hedge mustard **B** grows. It can be recognised by its branches, which often spread at right angles to the stem, its jagged leaves with points turned towards the stem, and the tiny,

pale yellow flowers only 2-3mm across which develop into vertical pods pressed close to the stem. Winter-cress **A** was, as the name suggests, once valued for salad in winter but was banished in favour of finer-flavoured vegetables. Common on stream banks, in ditches and other damp waste places, its yellow, wallflower-like flowers appear in a dense cluster in spring, which elongates as summer progresses into a spike of stalked, 4-angled pods.

A Winter-cress *Barbarea vulgaris*. Given this Latin name as it was once known as 'Herb St Barbara' after a saint whose day was in December when the leaves were most appreciated. Flowers May—August.

B Hedge mustard *Sisymbrium officinale*. Clusters of tiny flowers overtop the elongating stem; wiry skeletons of dead plants persist throughout winter. Flowers June—July.

C Rape *Brassica napus*. Various varieties grown for oil-seed or forage and escape onto roadsides and into waste places. Flowers May—August.

D Charlock *Sinapis arvensis*. Large seeds can persist in soil for 50 years and 'crops' of charlock occur when old pastures are ploughed or verges disturbed. Flowers May—July.

E Wild radish *Raphanus raphanistrum*. Also known as 'white charlock', but only apt in south-east England, as in north and west flowers may be yellow **Ea** or lilac with dark veins. Flowers May—September.

A

B

C

D

E

Ea

'Cabbages': white flowered 1

The wild garden can be a valuable source of salad vegetables and flavours at all seasons and the *Cruciferae* make a strong contribution with garlics, mustards and cresses. In most species the leaves are used but in one, horse-radish **A**, it is the root from which the sauce is made to give that distinctive additional flavour to roast beef. However, ancient beef-eaters must have gone without it because horse-radish was not introduced to this country from the Near East until the 15th century. It has since escaped from gardens into hedges and onto roadside verges and thence to river banks, where it is so well established it looks like a native species. But its white flowers rarely produce ripe pods in our climate and it is spread almost entirely by its roots or underground stems.

In true garlic the underground parts also provide the flavour but in garlic mustard **B** it is the heart-shaped leaves. When crushed, they give a strong smell of garlic and a few young leaves shredded into a salad produce the pleasures without the reprise of garlic itself. It is known also as 'Jack-by-the-hedge' because it most frequently forms long trails of white against the bright green, fresh-bursting leaves of a hawthorn hedge in spring.

Scurvygrass **D** also forms white patches in hedgerows, particularly in the west of Britain, but it is frequent too in salt marshes and on sea banks all round our coast, except the south east, and along mountain streams to over 900m. The leaves contain ascorbic acid and sailors suffering from the sores of scurvy found they could be cured by eating this herb.

No need to climb mountains for field penny cress **C**; it could be amongst the cabbages in the kitchen garden or in nearby arable land. It is unmistakeable when the tiny, white flowers are succeeded by pods about 3cm across (the size of an old penny and hence the plant's name) with a deep notch at the top **Ca**. The leaves are edible, in moderation, but their bitter aroma is not everybody's taste.

A Horse-radish *Amoracia rusticana*. Lower leaves often deeply cut like the teeth of a comb; upper are smaller and undivided. Flowers May—June.

B Garlic mustard *Alliaria petiolata*. Once valued for making a sauce for salt fish, hence name 'sauce alone' in Somerset. Flowers April—June.

C Field penny-cress *Thlaspi arvense*. Pods 3cm across in two parts attached to a central partition at right angles to the pod. Flowers May—July.

D Common scurvygrass *Cochlearia officinalis*. Pea-sized pods, the round central partition of which persists when seeds are shed. Flowers May—August.

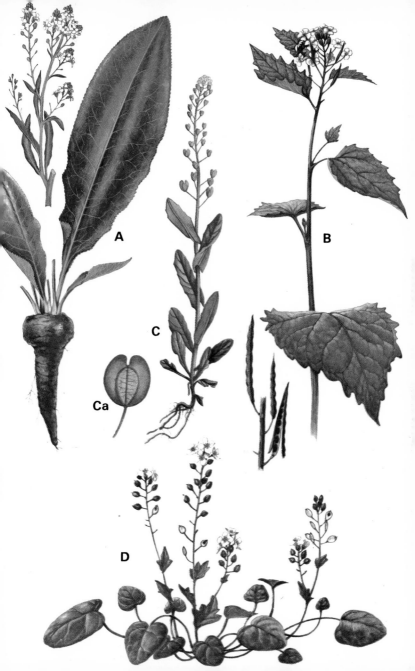

A

B

C

Ca

D

'Cabbages': white flowered 2

In the comparatively mild British winters some wild plants are in flower in the garden even in darkest December. One of the most reliable is shepherd's-purse **A**, recognised by the heart-shaped seed pods which resemble the purses carried round their waists by medieval shepherds. It is also known as 'pickpocket' or 'pickpurse' because it robs the farmer by stealing the goodness from his land.

As soon as the sun begins to warm the soil in spring the tiny white-flowered **Fa** annual whitlow-grass **F**, sometimes barely 2-3cm in height, may be found on old walls, gravel paths and other dry places like rocks and sand dunes. A few weeks later and often in the same habitat, the equally small-flowered, but much taller, thale-cress **D** comes into bloom. Both these annuals produce pods divided by a thin partition, the septum, which persists long after the minute seeds are shed — round or oval in whitlow-grass, long and narrow in thale-cress.

Hairy bitter-cress **E** also has long, narrow pods which, when ripe, have an explosive mechanism which flings the seeds some distance. This is often triggered off when brushed by a walker taking an amble down a gravel path, round sandpits or in dunes where it grows — a disturbing experience. Wavy bitter-cress **B** lacks these explosive pods and is a shade-loving annual of banks and stream sides, where it may be recognised by its zig-zag (wavy) stem with numerous stem leaves in contrast to hairy bitter-cress's straight stem and very few stem leaves.

Cuckooflower **C** is closely related to the bitter-cresses but is a perennial with petals three times as long as the sepals, which, though occasionally white, are normally lilac, colouring wet meadows and marshes in early spring.

Another perennial of damp places, even growing in streams, is the familiar salad vegetable, water-cress **G**. The white, 4-petalled flowers develop long sausage- or cucumber-shaped pods.

A Shepherd's-purse *Capsella bursa-pastoris*. Before flowers develop, can be recognised by rosette of leaves, outer ones pressed closely to ground. Flowers all year round.

B Wavy bitter-cress *Cardamine flexuosa*. Flowers have 6 stamens **Ba** compared with 4 in hairy bitter-cress **Ea** — remember *flex*=six. Flowers April—September.

C Cuckooflower *Cardamine pratensis*. Leaves are similar in shape and taste to water-cress and can be used in salads. Flowers April—June.

D Thale-cress *Arabidopsis thaliana*. Basal rosette of greyish-green leaves, often covered in branched hairs. Flowers April—May (sometimes also September—October).

E Hairy bitter-cress *Cardamine hirsuta*. Badly named because it is only slightly hairy, and wavy bitter-cress has hairier stems. Flowers April—August

F Common whitlow-grass *Erophila verna*. Pods vary: often rugby-ball shaped in gardens, football-shaped in dunes. Flowers March—June.

G Water-cress *Nasturtium officinale*. Grown for table in large beds, particularly along chalk streams in southern England. Flowers May—October.

A

B

Ba

C

D

E

Ea

F

Fa

G

Violets and pansies

There can hardly be a British garden without its clump of violets or a bed or two of pansies. Violets all have more or less heart-shaped leaves and usually blue or violet flowers with the lower petal developed into a characteristic sac-like spur. The exception is sweet violet **A**, which has white forms which are frequently cultivated. This is the most attractive and highly scented of the species which occur wild in Britain, and to quote Shakespeare's King John: 'To throw a perfume on the violet . . . Is wasteful and ridiculous excess.' The roots have medicinal properties: a decoction of the rootstock makes a mild cough mixture.

Sweet violet is one of the two wild species with hairs on the leaf stalks; they are short and turned down. The other species is the hairy violet **B** with longer, spreading hairs on the leaf stalk, very hairy leaves and scentless flowers. It is the common species of grassland and open woods on dry, lime-rich soils in England.

The species of grassland and woods on neutral and acid soils is common dog-violet **C**, which has hairless leaf stalks and dark blue-violet flowers with a fat, paler-coloured spur **Ca**. This spur character is the easiest way to distinguish it from the early dog-violet, in which the spur is the same colour as the petals and more slender **Da**. Not only does this flower two to three weeks earlier than the common dog-violet but it is usually found only in woods with lime-rich soils.

Pansies are related to violets, but their lateral petals are vertical, not spreading horizontally and the 'leaves' (stipules) on the stem are divided into conspicuous lobes. The showy flowers vary in colour, being blue-violet, yellow, cream or white, often combined in a single blossom. Wild pansy **E**, has large flowers, often nearly as large as the garden pansy which was derived from the wild species. It is also known as heartsease, but rather as a cure for love than physical heart diseases.

Field pansy **F** has flowers only about half the size; it is an annual of arable fields but frequently occurs in the kitchen garden, where its beauty should protect it from the hoe.

A Sweet violet *Viola odorata*. Spreads by long runners; open flowers usually infertile; later closed flowers produce seed. Flowers February—April.

B Hairy violet *Viola hirta*. No long runners; a small form with flowers less than 1cm (sub-species *calcarea*) grows in dry calcareous pastures. Flowers April—May.

C Common dog-violet *Viola riviniana*. In fruit, sepals have large appendages pointing towards stalk; spur of flower stout **Ca**. Flowers April—June.

D Early dog-violet *Viola reichenbachiana*. In fruit, appendages on sepals pointing towards stalk are very small: spur slender. Flowers March—May.

E Wild pansy *Viola tricolor*. Petals longer than sepals; mid-lobe of stipule narrow, untoothed. Flowers April—September.

F Field pansy *Viola arvensis*. Petals equalling or shorter than sepals; mid-lobe of stipule broad, toothed. Flowers April—October.

Rockroses and St John's-worts

No rock garden is complete without a collection of rockroses of many colours derived from common rockrose and from hybrids with white rockrose *Helianthemum apenninum*. Common rockrose **A** is a trailing, almost evergreen, perennial with opposite leaves, one of the delights of the chalk and limestone grassland of Britain, where its yellow 5-petalled flowers may be found throughout the summer. Rarer in the west, it is found in only one place in Ireland.

Tutsan **B** is also a semi-evergreen perennial with opposite leaves but it is upright and, in contrast to rockrose, is scarce, except as a garden escape, on the eastern side of Britain but common in the south and west and throughout Ireland. The leaves were once used to heal fresh wounds and it was called *'toute-sain'*, all heal, in Normandy, from which the English name is clearly derived.

About ten species of St John's-wort occur wild in Britain: they are all perennial herbs with alternating pairs of opposite leaves and 5-petalled, yellow flowers with abundant stamens.

Hairy St John's-wort **C** is the only species of dry places with hairs on both leaf surfaces. It has smooth stems and may be found in woods and scrubby grassland throughout England, except in the south west, and in eastern Scotland on lime-rich soils, especially when capped by clay. Slender St John's-wort **D** is a species of acid heath and grassland. It also has smooth stems but the rounded heart-shaped leaves are without hairs on either surface.

Common St John's-wort **E** has 2 raised lines on its stems, and leaves which, when picked and held up to the light, show many glandular dots which look like perforations. It occurs in open woods and grassland and is most abundant on lime-rich soils **Ea**.

Imperforate St John's-wort **F** has 4 raised lines on its stems, and leaves, which when held up to the light, show few or no perforations, hence its English name. Also found in open woods and grassland, it is uncommon on lime-rich soils.

A Common rockrose *Helianthemum nummularium*. Numerous stamens produce abundant pollen attracting insects; if pollination fails, flowers close at night or in wet weather and self-pollination occurs. Flowers June—September.

B Tutsan *Hypericum androsaemum*. Stems have 2 raised lines; leaves have strong resinous smell when crushed and persist throughout year. Flowers June—August.

C Hairy St John's-wort *Hypericum hirsutum*. Sepals and bracts (small 'leaves' amongst the flowers) with short-stalked, black glands on margins. Flowers July—August.

D Slender St John's-wort *Hypericum pulchrum*. Bases of opposite leaves clasp stem and overlap; sepals rounded, fringed with black glands. Flowers June—August.

E Common St John's-wort *Hypericum perforatum*. Sepals pointed, untoothed **Eb**; herb of St John the Baptist, gathered on the eve of St John's day (June 24) and hung in windows as protection from demons. Flowers June—September.

F Imperforate St John's-wort *Hypericum maculatum*. Sepals obtuse with coarse irregular teeth **Fa**; petals marked on outside with black vertical lines and dots. Flowers June—August.

A

B

C

D

Ea

Eb

E

Fa

F

Campions

Campions symbolise the champion, once being used in making floral wreaths with which to crown the winners at public games. And they do look 'right champion' in field or hedgerow but are striking enough to be grown for ornament in your own garden.

Bladder campion **A** is a common perennial on roadside banks and in other dry, grassy places and usually grows in distinct clumps. Readily recognised by its greyish-green hairless leaves arranged in opposite pairs, and the white flowers up to 2cm across with a remarkable inflated bladder-like calyx which encloses and hides the seed-bearing capsule **Aa**. Some of the flowers are male, some female whilst others are bisexual. They are fragrant and attract night-flying moths and long-tongued bees.

White campion **B** is often found with bladder campion but it is biennial and also grows as an arable weed. It is an upright plant with softly hairy leaves and handsome flowers up to 3cm across. These are fragrant and, when fully open in the evening, are easily visible to pollinating moths.

Though red campion **C** is also a hedgerow plant, it is more shade-tolerant than the other two species and is frequent in woods on lime-rich soils. Handsome enough to grace any garden, its rose-coloured flowers are over 2cm across, but scentless and adapted for pollination by butterflies, bees and long-tongued flies rather than moths.

Ideally a wildflower garden designed for insects should have both white and red campions. You may then have the excitement of observing the hybridisation which readily occurs, producing plants with many shades of pink flowers. But be careful — both these species have separate male and female plants and neither hybridisation nor continuation of the population will be achieved with plants of only one sex.

The jagged rose-red petals of ragged-robin **D**, a perennial of marshes, damp meadows and old woods, are unmistakable; each of the five petals is divided into four narrow segments. Though the name robin seems innocent, plants with robin names are often linked to goblins and evil, and it could be unlucky to pick the flowers and take them into the house — leave them in the garden with the gnomes. The specific name for the flower, *flos-cuculi*, comes from the Latin and means cuckoo-flower, for it flowers when cuckoos are calling.

A Bladder campion *Silene vulgaris.* Closely related sea campion has smaller leaves, shorter stems and larger flowers and occurs on rocky shores. Flowers June—August.

B White campion *Silene alba.* Capsule almost 1cm across with narrow opening at the top, surrounded by 10 teeth. Flowers May—September.

C Red campion *Silene dioica.* Capsule 7–8mm across with broad opening at the top surrounded by 10 down-curled teeth. Flowers May—July.

D Ragged-robin *Lychnis flos-cuculi.* Capsule only 5mm across, with 5 down-turned teeth; whole plant reddish in colour. Flowers May—June.

Chickweeds, mouse-ears and stitchworts

This group of small herbs rarely more than 30cm high is easily recognised by their untoothed, opposite leaves, white flowers with 5 white petals notched at the tip so deeply that there appear to be 10, although there are usually 10 stamens. Mouse-ears have ovaries with 5 styles (whereas chickweeds and stitchworts have only 3); these ovaries develop into 10 toothed capsules.

Common mouse-ear **B** is frequent in gardens, where it forms dark green patches on the lawn, and in grassland throughout Britain. Another perennial 'mouse-ear' in most gardens is snow-in-summer **E** with larger flowers and white-felted leaves: it spreads all too rapidly, swamping smaller species in the rockery, and becomes established in hedgebanks.

There are three widespread annual mouse-ears. All are densely covered in glands to which soil or sand adhere. The commonest, which occurs on garden paths or in the potato patch, is sticky mouse-ear **C**, with flowers clustered on short stalks at the top of the stem. In sea mouse-ear **A** and little mouse-ear **D** the flowers are not clustered but grow on stalks longer than the sepals: the capsules which develop on the former are held upright whereas those of the latter often turn down. Common chickweed **I** also has down-turned capsules: an annual, it is perhaps the commonest wild flower in the garden, forming large grass-green patches amongst the vegetables and can grow and flower throughout the year.

Three stitchworts are common throughout the British Isles: great stitchwort **G** found in hedgerows and woods; lesser stitchwort **H** of heaths and dry grassland; and bog stitchwort

F of bogs, marshes and wet woods.

A Sea mouse-ear *Cerastium diffusum*. Usually 4 petals, bracts leafy; in stony and sandy places near the sea, rarely inland. Flowers May—July.

B Common mouse-ear *Cerastium fontanum*. Pairs of opposite, hairy leaves which look a little like the ears of mice. Flowers April—September.

C Sticky mouse-ear *Cerastium glomeratum. Glomerate* refers to way flowers glomerate or are clustered at top of stems. Flowers April—September.

D Little mouse-ear *Cerastium semidecandrum*. 5 petals, bracts with broad, white margins; dry sandy and calcareous soils, only coastal in west. Flowers April—May.

E Snow-in-summer *Cerastium tomentosum*. Also called 'dusty miller': large, white flowers and white, felted leaves are origin of these names. Flowers May—August.

F Bog stitchwort *Stellaria alsine*. Petals shorter than sepals make tiny, deeply divided flowers (6mm) look like white-centred, green stars; leaves elliptical. Flowers May—July.

G Great stitchwort *Stellaria holostea*. Flowers up to 2–3cm across with petals twice as long as the sepals and notched to halfway; leaves long and narrow with rough margins. Flowers April—June.

H Lesser stitchwort *Stellaria graminea*. Flowers up to 1cm across with petals slightly longer than sepals and notched almost to the base; leaves long and narrow with smooth margins. Flowers May—August.

I Common chickweed *Stellaria media*. Rather juicy stems have a simple line of hairs which changes sides at each pair of leaves. Flowers all year round.

Pearlworts and sandworts

Pearlworts are small herbs rarely more than 15cm high with narrow bristle-like leaves, of which two species commonly occur in gardens.

Procumbent pearlwort **D** is a mat-forming perennial with a short, central, non-flowering stem, bearing a central leaf rosette and with flowers arising from procumbent, rooting, lateral stems. It is a widespread weed in garden paths, cracks in paving and in old lawns, which also occurs in grassland throughout Britain, especially in damp places by streams.

Annual pearlwort **C** forms upright tufts and has no central, non-flowering stem or procumbent, rooting, lateral stems. It also occurs 'down the garden path', especially when of gravel, and also in dry, open habitats like disused railway platforms.

Sandworts are small, much-branched annuals rarely more than 20cm high with small, white 5-petalled flowers and pairs of opposite leaves similar to chickweed and mouse-ear but the petals are neither notched or divided.

Three-nerved sandwort **B** is a spreading herb with many delicate trailing branches; the lower leaves are small and stalked, the upper larger and stalkless, and, if held up to the light, show clearly the three veins running from base to tip which give the plant its name. It is a shade-lover of dry woods and copses.

Thyme-leaved sandwort **A** is a more compact, upright plant with smaller leaves, rarely exceeding 6mm in length, which grows in sunny, open places like old quarries and sand dunes and may even occur on top of a garden wall.

Corn spurrey **E** is a scrambling plant about 30cm high, covered in sticky glandular hairs with long, narrow leaves arranged in clusters at the swollen joints of the stem. Its 5 white un-notched petals are slightly longer than the sepals **Ea**; flowers develop into capsules on stalks which turn down when they are ripe. A troublesome weed of cornfields and bare ground, it occurs especially where the soil is light and sandy.

A Thyme-leaved sandwort *Arenaria serpyllifolia*. Recognised in fruit by flask-shaped capsule longer than clasping sepals with 6 upright teeth. Flowers June—August.

B Three-nerved sandwort *Moehringia trinervia*. In fruit the rounded capsule is shorter than surrounding, not clasping, sepals and has 4—6 downwardly curved teeth **Bb**. Flowers May—June.

C Annual pearlwort *Sagina apetala*. 4 minute petals often fall early; flower stalks glandular and hairy; capsule equalling horizontally held sepals **Ca**. Flowers May—August.

D Procumbent pearlwort *Sagina procumbens*. 4—5 minute petals (often none); flower stalks hairless; capsule longer than horizontally held sepals **Da**. Flowers May—September.

E Corn spurrey *Spergula arvensis*. Grown as crop in some parts of Europe; fed to sheep, gives fine flavour to mutton. Flowers June—August.

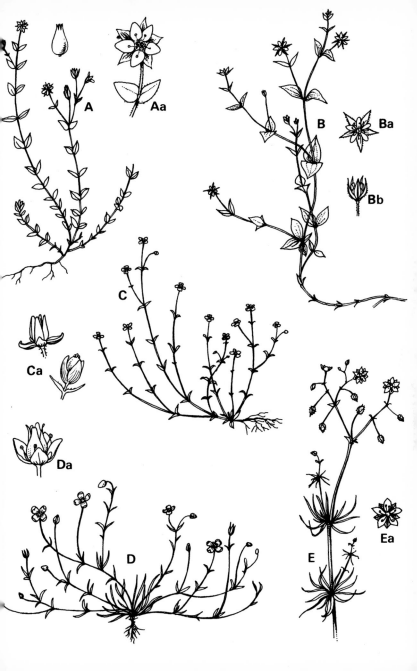

Goosefoots and oraches

The goosefoot family is distinguished by its small, green flowers with 3 to 5 'perianth' segments (there are no separate petals and sepals). Many have a mealy appearance as if sprinkled with flour. Several species are cultivated in the kitchen garden, including spinach, beetroot and, occasionally, Good-King-Henry, whilst a number of annuals turn up as weeds.

Oraches are odd in having separate male and female flowers, the former with, usually, 5 perianth segments but the latter with none, though the ovary is enclosed in two bracts or small leaves which enlarge after flowering in late summer and develop large warts on the outside. Two species are widespread in gardens and as weeds in arable land. Common orache **A** has the upper leaves of the stem oblong and tapering into the stalk, whereas spear-leaved orache **B**, as the name suggests, has all its leaves shaped like a spearhead. Both species are also common in waste places by the sea.

About 15 species of goosefoot, all rather similar in appearance, occur in waste places. They have 5 perianth segments and hermaphrodite (male and female together) flowers.

By far the commonest, and to be expected in every garden or allotment, is fat-hen **C**. A very mealy plant with triangular leaves and clusters of smallish, green flowers, it is similar to spear-leaved orache but can be distinguished because, whereas the oraches have the lowest branches opposite, in fat-hen and other goosefoots they are alternate.

Red goosefoot **D** is frequent in the south and east of Britain, where it is found especially round farm-yards, manure heaps and other places, like sewage farms, with a high nitrogen concentration. It is similar to fat-hen but the whole plant has a reddish tinge.

Good-King-Henry **E** is a perennial, spinach-like plant with spear-shaped leaves and spikes of tiny, greenish-white flowers. Grown in old-fashioned gardens as a pot-herb and often found as a throw-out on roadsides, the young shoots can be boiled and eaten with butter.

A Common orache *Atriplex patula*. Leaves mealy on both sides, lower ones toothed but never spear-like; bracteoles in fruit scarcely toothed. Flowers July—September.

B Spear-leaved orache *Atriplex hastata*. Leaves mealy only on underside, all spear-like; bracteoles in fruit toothed all round margins. Flowers July—September.

C Fat-hen *Chenopodium album*. Formerly valued for food: seeds were eaten with other grain and leaves taken boiled and mixed with butter. Flowers July—October.

D Red goosefoot *Chenopodium rubrum*. Named goosefoot from this species; broad, triangular leaf with coarsely toothed margin supposed to resemble foot of a goose. Flowers June—September.

E Good-King-Henry *Chenopodium bonus-henricus*. Seems to have acquired its name to distinguish it from Bad Henry, another name for poisonous dog's mercury. Flowers May—July.

Flaxes and mallows

Blue fields of flax **A** were once a feature of the summer landscape when the plant was cultivated for the production of linen fibre from its stems or linseed oil from the ripe seeds. Formerly found on roadsides as a relic from this cultivation, it is now mainly seen on rubbish tips, waste ground and in gardens where it has been introduced with cage-birdseed.

Fairy flax **B** is a dainty little annual of old grassland, especially chalk and limestone, and of moors and sand dunes. It is easily recognised by its thin, wiry, many-branched stems, opposite leaves and tiny white 5-petalled flowers, which develop into the typical 5-celled capsule of the flax family **Ba**. Also called 'purging flax' because of its laxative properties, the stems were bruised before boiling in white wine, and peppermint was sometimes added to disguise the bitter flavour.

The mallow family produces many popular garden plants, including hibiscus and hollyhock. Wild mallows have large, showy flowers and should be encouraged if they invade our herbaceous borders. Each flower has 5 notched petals which surround a central column containing anthers and stigmas. The distinctive calyx has an outer ring of 3 'leaves' attached to the lower part of the true calyx, which has five broad lobes.

Common mallow **D** has blue or purple flowers up to 4cm across and rounded leaves and is common on roadsides and in waste places throughout the lowlands. The fruits are a disc of nutlets resembling a flat cake or cheese which are edible, hence local names like 'fairy cheese' or 'bread and cheese'. They actually taste like peanuts.

Musk mallow **C** is a most handsome plant with rose-pink or white flowers over 4cm across and deeply divided, feathery leaves. It grows wild in hedges and on woodland margins, deriving its name from the peculiar smell it gives off when kept in a warm, confined space.

A Flax *Linum usitatissimum*. Leaves linear, spirally arranged; petals 1·5cm. Pale flax (*Linum bienne*), with smaller petals (about 1cm), is a native of dry grassland in south and west Britain. Flowers May—September.

B Fairy flax *Linum catharticum*. Leaves oblong with blunt tips, in opposite pairs; flowers less than 1cm across. Flowers June—September.

C Musk mallow *Malva moschata*. Leaves at bottom of stem kidney-shaped and long-stalked, becoming successively shorter stalked and more deeply divided going up the stem. Flowers July—August.

D Common mallow *Malva sylvestris*. Valued medicinally for the mucilage it contains; leaves used for poultices and roots to make a soothing ointment. Flowers June—October.

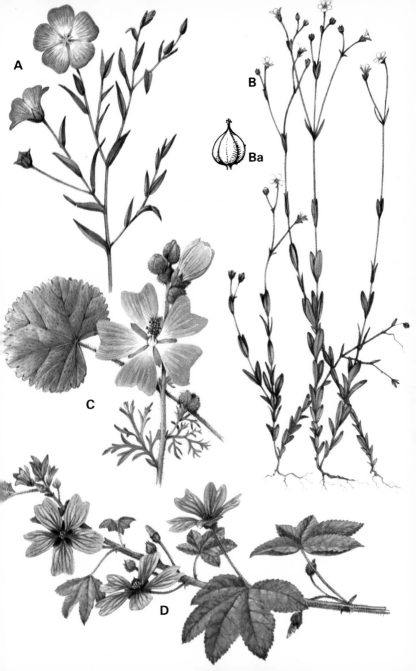

A

B

Ba

C

D

Crane's-bills and stork's-bills

Crane's-bills and stork's-bills are members of the geranium family which includes the geraniums of our summer gardens belonging to the genus *Pelargonium*, distinguished by their irregular flowers with spurs attached to the flower stalks.

Crane's-bills are frequent on roadside verges and in old grassland. They have rounded leaves and flowers varying in colour from pink to violet-blue. These flowers are normally in pairs with 10 stamens and 5 petals, narrowing at the base to a point or claw. The English name refers to the long, central beak of the fruit, which has 5 one-seeded lobes and when ripe the outer wall of each lobe springs up, flinging out the seed.

There are four widespread annual crane's-bills, usually under 30cm high with leaves less than 4cm across and pinkish petals never longer than 1cm. Dove's-foot crane's-bill **D** is so named because of the softness of its leaves, which have lobes divided about two-thirds of the distance between the margin and the central stalk. Small-flowered crane's-bill **E** is similar but the flowers have only 5–7 stamens, 3–5 without anthers. Cut-leaved crane's-bill **C**, as the name suggests, has leaves divided almost to the stalk, but can also be recognised by its long-awned sepals **Ca**. Shining crane's-bill **F** can also be identified by its leaves, which are hairless, a bright, glossy green and divided only about half-way to the stalk.

There are two widespread perennial species on roadside verges: meadow crane's-bill **H** colours long stretches in summer, having violet-blue petals strongly marked with crimson veins, whereas hedgerow crane's-bill **G** has smaller, often paler flowers in which the petals are deeply notched.

Herb Robert **B** is recognised by its much divided leaves, often tinged with red, and a strong 'geranium' smell.

Common stork's-bill **A** differs from crane's-bill in two ways: its leaves divide into opposite pairs of leaflets and segments of the beak do not roll upwards but twist spirally.

A Common stork's-bill *Erodium cicutarium*. Petals often have black spot at base and fall very easily; sand-loving species of dunes near sea and dry heaths inland. Flowers June—September.

B Herb robert *Geranium robertianum*. Common in woods and shady hedge banks but also on rocks and seashore shingle, when whole plant is deep red. Flowers May—September.

C Cut-leaved crane's-bill *Geranium dissectum*. Flowers with slightly notched petals on 1cm individual stalks; found in meadows, hedge banks and waste ground. Flowers May—August.

D Dove's-foot crane's bill *Geranium molle*. Hairs on stems of two kinds: short are glandular, long eglandular **Da**; all 10 stamens with anthers. Flowers April—September.

E Small-flowered crane's-bill *Geranium pusillum*. Hairs on stems all short, eglandular **Ea**; 5 stamens without anthers. Flowers June—September.

F Shining crane's-bill *Geranium lucidum*. Sepals with long-awned tips; frequent on limestone walls and banks. Flowers May—August.

G Hedgerow crane's-bill *Geranium pyrenaicum*. Introduced from mountains of Spain and Portugal but only found on lowland roadsides in this country. Flowers June—August.

H Meadow crane's-bill *Geranium pratense*. Flowering stalks turn down after flowering, re-erect in ripe fruit; leaves divided almost to base. Flowers June—September.

A

B

C

Ca

Da

D

Ea

E

F

G

H

Pea flowers: clovers, trefoils and medick

These members of the pea family are easily recognised by having their leaves divided into 3 (hence trefoil and *Trifolium*) and their flowers in spherical clusters.

There are over 20 species of clover in Britain, of which two perennials, red clover and white clover, are widely sown as fodder plants and may be found in most meadows and old grassland. They are also important to beekeepers: their nectar attracts bees which are essential for pollination, their weight being necessary to operate a mechanism which brushes pollen on their abdomens.

White clover **D** occurs in lawns, where its creeping habit and ability to root from spreading stems make it resistant to mowing. Red clover **E** is a more upright plant. Commonly in meadows, rarely in lawns, it may be confused with zig-zag clover, *Trifolium medium* (not illustrated). They are not easily distinguished but the latter has zig-zag stems, narrower leaflets and flatter, redder heads of flowers.

Trefoils are annual clovers with pale yellow flowers which are found in grassland and disturbed soils. Hop trefoil **C** is the larger of two common species, with heads of about 40 flowers which look like miniature hop cones, especially when brown and withered: it is most frequent in open, disturbed chalk or limestone soils. Lesser trefoil **B**

has only about 20 flowers in each head and may colour old lawns yellow when the daisy days are over. It is often confused with black medick **A** but can be distinguished by the absence of a protruding central nerve in its leaflets **Aa**, **Ba** and by its paler yellow flowers, which turn down as they wither. Both species are sold as shamrock, but barrow boys are not botanists. Medicks differ from clovers in having pods which are not straight but are sickle-shaped or spirally coiled.

A Black medick *Medicago lupulina*. Yellow flowers devop small, 1-seeded, black, sickle-shaped pods; sown as a crop with grass and clover. Flowers April—August.

B Lesser trefoil *Trifolium dubium*. Pale yellow flowers turn dark brown and develop into straight, light brown, 2-seeded pods. Flowers May—October.

C Hop trefoil *Trifolium campestre*. Lemon-yellow flowers turn light brown; seeds yellow, rather shiny. Flowers June—September.

D White clover *Trifolium repens*. Leaflets often heart-shaped, usually with a whitish, angled band towards base. Flowers June—September.

E Red clover *Trifolium pratense*. Leaflets elliptical, sometimes notched at tip, usually with whitish, crescent-shaped spot towards base. Flowers May—September.

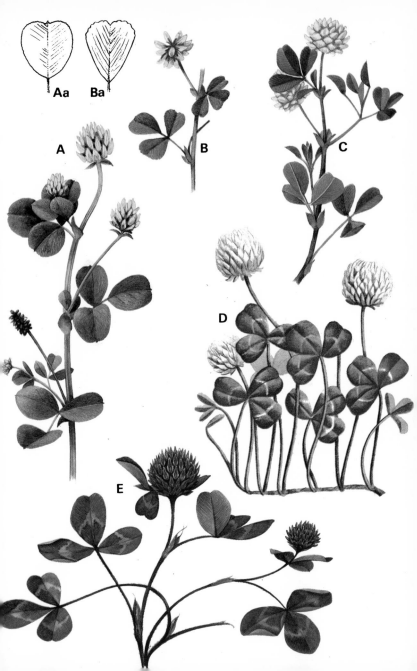

Pea flowers: tares, vetches and vetchlings

This group of climbing or scrambling herbs is distinguished by their sweet-pea-like flowers and leaves with one to many pairs of opposite leaflets and a terminal, usually branched, tendril which twines around bushes, etc.

There are two common vetchlings which differ from the other species in having only one or two pairs of leaflets and a winged or angled stem; the function of the leaves is partly taken over by enlarged 'stipules' (leaf-like structures on stem at base of leaf stalk).

The commoner is meadow vetchling **B** with pale yellow flowers and one pair of leaflets and it is found in hedgerows and rough undergrazed grassland. Bitter vetchling **A** usually has two pairs of leaflets and crimson flowers which brighten many dark woods, thickets and shady hedge banks, especially in upland areas. It has thick tuberous underground stems.

Four kinds of vetch are common and widespread in Britain. Common vetch **F** was once widely grown as a fodder crop and may still be found in and around fields and roadsides. Its purple flowers about 2-3cm long with paler petals above are in ones or twos at the base of the leaves. Narrow-leaved vetch **E** is similar but smaller: the flowers only 1cm long with all petals bright pink. Both distinguished from others by a black spot on the underside of the stipule.

The other two common vetches are perennials. Bush vetch **H** has purple flowers in groups of 2–6 on short stems and almost hairless leaves: it has strongly growing underground stems and can be difficult to eradicate. Tufted vetch **G** has hairy, somewhat greyish leaves and striking blue flowers in dense spikes of up to 40 on long stalks.

Though tares may have adulterated the wheat in biblical times, they are not usually arable weeds in Britain. There are two of these slender summer-flowering annuals which are common in long grass. Smooth tare **C** has smooth 4-seeded pods and pale blue flowers whereas hairy tare **D** has hairy 2-seeded pods and dirty white flowers; abundant on old railway lines.

A Bitter vetchling *Lathyrus montanus*. Stipules at base of leaf small, shaped like half an arrow head. Flowers April—July.

B Meadow vetchling *Lathyrus pratensis*. Stipules at base of leaf larger than in bitter vetchling (up to 2cm long), shaped like whole arrow head. Flowers May—August.

C Smooth tare *Vicia tetrasperma*. 4-seeded hairless pods; 2 calyx teeth shorter than the others; mainly on heavy clay soils. Flowers May—August.

D Hairy tare *Vicia hirsuta*. 2-seeded hairy pods **Da**; all calyx teeth of equal length; on dry soils of all kinds. Flowers May—August.

E Narrow-leaved vetch *Vicia angustifolia*. Pods 2–3cm long without constrictions between seeds; leaflets narrow with both acute and obtuse tips. Flowers May—September.

F Common vetch *Vicia sativa*. Pods 5–7cm long with constrictions between seeds **Fa**; leaflets broad with obtuse notched tips. Flowers May—September.

G Tufted vetch *Vicia cracca*. Leaves usually 10 or more pairs of greyish leaflets; ripe pods less than 8mm long. Flowers June—September.

H Bush vetch *Vicia sepium*. Leaves usually 5–9 pairs of almost hairless leaflets; ripe pods about 2–3cm long. Flowers May—August.

A

B

C

Da

D

E

Fa

F

G

H

Other pea flowers

Kidney vetch **A** is a handsome perennial which carpets our coasts in early summer but is also abundant in limestone and chalk grassland inland. The pom-pom-like heads are made of a cluster of red and yellow 'pea' flowers embedded in their woolly sepals.

Common bird's-foot trefoil **B**, which colours meadows and roadside verges everywhere, is ill-named because the hairless leaves are not trifoliate, as in clover, but have 5 leaflets. Simply bird's-foot might be a more accurate name — the heads of the stalked pea-like flowers are usually in groups of 4 or 5 which develop into pods arranged like the toes of a bird's foot.

Greater bird's-foot trefoil **C**, a less common plant of damp, marshy places, has hairy leaves and a hairy calyx with downturned teeth: there are usually 8 or more flowers in a head.

Melitots are tall annual or biennial herbs 60–120cm high with toothed, trifoliate leaves. The two commonest species have spikes of yellow flowers which develop into short, thick pods. In tall melitot **D** these pods are hairy and become black when ripe, whereas in common melitot **E** the pods are hairless, becoming brown and strongly wrinkled when ripe. Melitots have been much valued as herbs, being the chief ingredient of melitot poultice. When dried, they smell of new-mown hay because of the coumarin in their leaves.

Common restharrow **G** is so named because it has underground stems which are so tough they could bring the horse-drawn plough or harrow to a stop. Also called 'cammock', its leaves give off a nasty, goat-like smell when rubbed which can get into milk of grazing cows and give it an unpleasant taste: cheese so tainted was called cammocky.

Spiny restharrow **F** is similar but has no underground stems. The above-ground stems are usually spiny with 2 vertical rows of hairs, not hairy all round like common restharrow. It is particularly abundant on heavy clay soils in south and east England.

A Kidney vetch *Anthyllis vulneraria*. Valueless for curing kidney complaints but once widely used as a vulnerary to staunch bleeding, a property of many plants with downy leaves. Flowers June—September.

B Common bird's-foot-trefoil *Lotus corniculatus*. Stems solid or with narrow hollow at base; upper pair of teeth of almost hairless calyx divided by obtuse angle. Flowers June—September.

C Greater bird's-foot-trefoil *Lotus uliginosus*. Stems hollow; upper pair of teeth of hairy calyx divided by acute angle. Flowers June—August.

D Tall melilot *Melilotus altissima*. The lower petal (the keel) same length as wings on each side and standard above; pod hairy. Flowers June—August.

E Common melilot *Melilotus officinalis*. Lower petal shorter than wings and standard **Ea**; pod hairless **Eb**. Flowers July—August.

F Spiny restharrow *Ononis spinosa*. Leaflets over three times as long as broad; stems with hairs in 2 distinct rows. Flowers June—September.

G Common restharrow *Ononis repens*. Leaflets less than three times as long as broad; stems hairy all round. Flowers June—September.

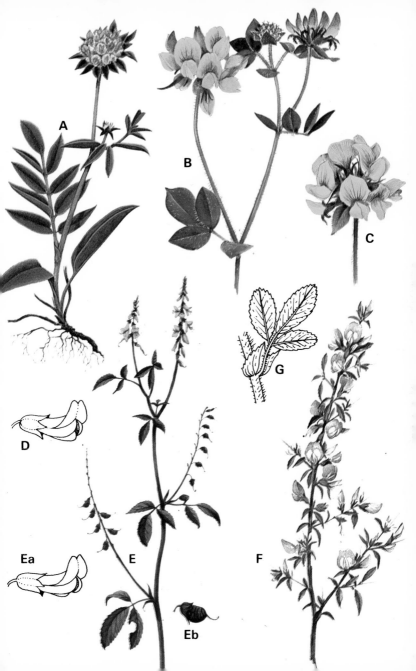

Strawberries and cinquefoils

Before the introduction of the garden strawberry, which is descended from two wild American species, people in this country used to cultivate the wild strawberry **A**. The berries are much smaller and a lot of labour is needed to pick a mouthful but the effort is worthwhile, for the flavour is sweeter than the cultivated varieties. Wild strawberries occur in scrub, open woods and hedgerows throughout the British Isles, especially on lime-rich soils where their white flowers first appear in April.

Barren strawberry **B** also has white flowers (some as early as February) but, like the other species of the genus *Potentilla*, it never produces succulent fruits. Though the leaves are similar to wild strawberry's, they can be distinguished by their blue-green colour and by having spreading hairs beneath.

Nearly all other wild species of *Potentilla* in Britain have yellow flowers. The most easily recognised is silverweed **C** with its much divided silky-hairy leaves; they are usually silvery on both sides but look out for specimens with hair on the underside only or with no 'silver' at all. The roots are edible and, before the introduction of the potato, this plant was cultivated in the west of Scotland. Roots were roasted or boiled, or dried and ground into meal for making bread or porridge.

Creeping cinquefoil **D** has five-fingered leaves from which comes its 'franglais' name. It has long runners like a strawberry and gardeners unfortunate enough to have it invading the rockery may give it other unprintable names. In the Middle Ages it was reputed to have magical powers and was hung over doors to keep out witches.

Tormentil **E** is a trailing herb similar to creeping cinquefoil but with the upper leaves divided into 3, not 5, and with most of the flowers having 4, rather than 5, petals. It is a common plant of poor soil on grasslands, heaths and bogs, in contrast to the cinquefoil which is most abundant on dry, lime-rich soils. The woody roots used to be boiled in milk and the liquid was given to children to relieve the torment of stomach-ache — hence its English name.

A Wild strawberry *Fragaria vesca*. Terminal tooth of leaflets longer than those on each side; petals touch each other or overlap **Aa**. Flowers April—July.

B Barren strawberry *Potentilla sterilis*. Terminal tooth of leaflets equalling or shorter than those on each side; petals do not touch each other. Flowers February—May.

C Silverweed *Potentilla anserina*. Spreads by overground runners to form large patches; scientific name, *anser* (goose), suggests it grows in grass where geese graze. Flowers June—August.

D Creeping cinquefoil *Potentilla reptans*. Outer calyx segments oval with inner segments, parts of flowers arranged in fives. Flowers June—September.

E Tormentil *Potentilla erecta*. Outer calyx segments much narrower than inner segments, parts of flowers normally in fours. Flowers June—September.

Stonecrops and saxifrages

No rock garden would be complete without its complement of stonecrops — creeping plants with upright flowering stems producing a spike or plate of white or yellow 5-petalled flowers during the heat of summer. They have spirally arranged, succulent leaves which store water, enabling them to grow on dry rocks, cliffs and walls where the water supply is limited and infrequently replenished.

Three species are commonly grown in gardens, only one of them is native but the other two frequently escape and become naturalised. The commonest in gardens and in the wild is the native yellow-flowered biting stonecrop **D** or wall-pepper, so named because of the acrid taste of its egg-shaped, overlapping, yellow-green leaves and its frequency on walls (and roofs); in the wild it is most abundant on sandy soils especially dunes near the sea. The other yellow common garden species is reflexed stonecrop **C**, a taller plant with pointed, spreading, dark-green leaves; introduced long ago from southern Europe.

The most widespread white-flowered species, white stonecrop **E** was also introduced from southern Europe. It has leaves 6–12cm long and a much-branched flowering stem and should not be confused with the native English stonecrop (not illustrated) which occurs on acid rocks, especially near the sea in western Britain: it has leaves less than 6mm in length and a flowering stem with only two main branches.

Another 5-petalled, white flower of the rock garden which may have been brought in with the rock, if it is limestone, is rue-leaved saxifrage **B**, an annual with 3-fingered basal leaves, often tinged with red. The closely related opposite-leaved golden-saxifrage **A** can instantly be recognised by its bright yellowish-green flowers. The colour is provided by bracts and sepals — there are no petals. This early-flowering species grows in wet woods and along streams, often showing the source of a mountain stream from a distance.

A Opposite-leaved golden-saxifrage *Chrysosplenium oppositifolium*. Eaten in salads in the Vosges region of eastern France under name of *'cresson du roche'*. Flowers April—July.

B Rue-leaved saxifrage *Saxifraga tridactylites*. Upper leaves often toothed; in very dry places tiny plants may produce only one flower and glandular hairy fruit. Flowers April—June.

C Reflexed stonecrop *Sedum reflexum*. Flowers in umbel-like heads; leaves up to 2cm long, pointed, at right-angles to stem or turned down (reflexed). Flowers June—August.

D Biting stonecrop *Sedum acre*. Flowers on only 2 or 3 main branches; leaves under 6mm long, blunt, covering each other, especially at stem base. Flowers June—July.

E White stonecrop *Sedum album*. Frequent on roofs where this and other species were planted as protection against lightning. Flowers June—August.

A

B

C

D

E

Willowherbs

These perennial herbs have willow-like leaves varying from long and narrow to heart-shaped. Distinguished by their rose or pink flowers with their parts arranged in fours, excepting the stamens of which there are 8. Each flower seems to be on a long stalk but this is an undeveloped fruit which, when the petals fall, elongates into a seed pod. The pod has 4 segments which unpeel from the top, exposing numerous seeds, each with a cottony 'parachute' which helps wind dispersal. Plants are also spread by vigorous over- or underground stems. This ability to spread to new areas is demonstrated by the two common species which most often turn up in our gardens now but which were rare or unknown in Britain a hundred years ago.

Rosebay willowherb **A** was rare as a native but suddenly began to spread about 1860 and is now everywhere except in the west of Ireland, and is particularly abundant round bonfire sites in cleared woodland — hence its other name 'fireweed'. Its flowers face sideways with lower petals smaller and leaves spirally arranged. Other species have their flowers facing upwards with four equal petals and lower leaves in opposite pairs.

American willowherb **B** was introduced from North America in 1891 and is found throughout lowland Britain. It has reddish stems covered in stalked glandular hairs and small flowers (up to 1cm across) with petals divided to half way **Ba**.

Broad-leaved willowherb **E** is most easily recognised by its leaves, which are egg shaped and short stalked. The commonest species in woods, it is also a frequent weed of rock garden and walls.

If there is a stream or river at the bottom of the garden, its banks are almost certain to be lined by great willowherb **C**, which grows up to 2m high, with distinctive deep-rose flowers up to 2–3cm across with a clear white, cross-shaped stigma in the centre.

Hoary willowherb **D** occurs in similar habitats but is smaller, rarely over 1m, with paler flowers up to 1cm across.

A Rosebay willowherb *Epilobium angustifolium*. Spreads rapidly by wind-blown plumed seeds and vigorous underground roots; long style, with lobed stigma, hangs down between lower petals. Flowers July—Sept.

B American willowherb *Epilobium ciliatum*. Commonest species of towns and gardens with club-shaped (unlobed) stigma; flowers wide open with petals horizontal. Flowers June—August.

C Great willowherb *Epilobium hirsutum*. Large white-lobed stigma visible across stream it grows by; densely covered in glandular and soft, spreading hairs; leaves clasp stem. Flowers July—August.

D Hoary willowherb *Epilobium parviflorum*. Lobed stigma not visible from distance; covered in short, soft, spreading hairs but only towards top; leaves not clasping stem. Flowers July—August.

E Broad-leaved willowherb *Epilobium montanum*. Recognised by lobed stigma, almost hairless stems and broad, opposite pairs of toothed leaves on very short stalks. Flowers June—August.

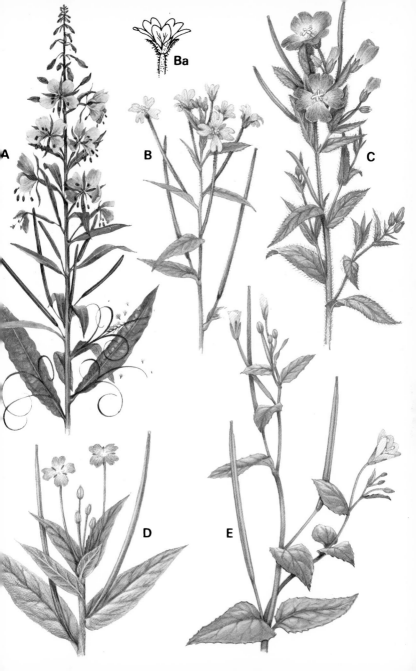

A

Ba

B

C

D

E

Parsley family (umbellifers) 1

Second only perhaps to mint, more of us grow members of the Parsley family for flavouring our food than any other herb. There can scarcely be a garden without a patch of parsley but the more adventurous may have chervil, dill, fennel and lovage in the herb bed, whilst no kitchen garden would be complete without roots of carrot and parsnip.

Many of these cultivated plants, like carrot and parsnip, have been developed from wild origins **A** and **B**, while others such as fennel **C** brought into our gardens have returned the compliment by escaping to the wild.

The scientific name of the family is the clue to its most obvious characteristic — Umbelliferae comes from the Latin *umbella*, the same origin as umbrella, and is a clear reference to the way in which the flowers are arranged on stalks like the ribs of an umbrella.

On the vegetable plot you may well find a 'parsley' you did not sow, the leaves of which are highly poisonous but look a little like parsley. No doubt because children, sent out for a sprig for the sauce, have brought back *Aethusa cynapium* by mistake, its English name is fool's parsley **D**.

If you are very unlucky another umbel may have invaded your rockery or herbaceous border and be impossible to get rid of. Variously known as goat-weed, gout-weed, bishop-weed, ground-elder **E** and, in Northern Ireland, as garden plague, it was originally introduced in medieval times as a pot-herb or a cure for gout, and has long outstayed its welcome. Those who give up the struggle may eat its leaves boiled as a kind of spicy spinach.

A Wild carrot *Daucus carota*. Crushed leaves smell of carrot; bracts at base of umbel are much divided; stems and fruits are very hairy. Flowers June—August.

B Wild parsnip *Pastinaca sativa*. Leaves smell of parsnip; no bracts or bracteoles at base of lower or upper 'umbrellas'; stems hairy. Flowers July—August.

C Fennel *Foeniculum vulgare*. Crushed leaves smell of 'cough-mixture'; no little leaves (bracts or bracteoles) at base of lower or upper 'umbrellas'; stems are solid. Flowers July—October.

D Fool's parsley *Aethusa cynapium*. Long, streamer-like bracteoles hang below upper 'umbrellas', but bracts absent; fruits round, shining. POISONOUS. Flowers June—September.

E Ground-elder *Aegopodium podagraria*. Creeping perennial with large, lobed leaves; bracts and bracteoles absent. Flowers May—June.

Parsley family 2

Follow a barge-horse's hoof-steps along the tow-path and you may feel like Alice beneath the mushroom, as gigantic umbels rise above your head — but eschew any signs saying 'eat me' because most of them could be extremely poisonous. Commonest and tallest found here (up to 3m) look for hemlock **A** on the landward side, a species with spotted stems. (The tallest umbel which grows wild in Britain is giant hogweed which can reach over 4m.) The equally poisonous hemlock water-dropwort **B** occurs on the water side and its leaves have been eaten in mistake for celery with tragic consequences; but celery has no bracts or bracteoles whereas hemlock water-dropwort has both.

Wild angelica **C** may occur with either of these hemlocks. It is almost as tall, but much stouter with purplish leaves and stems — this is not poisonous and the closely related garden angelica is cultivated for its aromatic leaf stalks used in cake-making.

Down at the water's edge, the simply divided leaves of fool's water-cress **E** could be mistaken for the real thing but, in flower, it is unmistakeable with bractless umbels on very short stalks opposite a leaf. It might, however, be confused with lesser water-parsnip **D**, with simply divided leaves and umbels with bracts, usually divided into several segments.

A Hemlock *Conium maculatum*. Purple spotted, hairless stem usually covered in waxy bloom; leaves fern-like; fruits small and round. POISONOUS. Flowers June—July.

B Hemlock water-dropwort *Oenanthe crocata*. Roots have cylindrical ovoid tubers which are sweet to taste but very POISONOUS to humans and cattle. Flowers June—July.

C Wild angelica *Angelica sylvestris*. No bracts at base of lower 'umbrellas'; upper leaves with inflated stalk and few or no leaflets above. Flowers July—September.

D Lesser water-parsnip *Berula erecta*. Leaves usually with 5—9 pairs of leaflets and purple ring towards bottom of leaf stalk; bracts at base of lower 'umbrellas' divided into 3—5 lobes. Flowers July—September.

E Fool's water-cress *Apium nodiflorum*. Leaves with 4—6 pairs of leaflets. No bracts but bracteoles present. Flowers July—September.

Parsley family 3

The parsley family dominates our roadsides from May to September. In May thousands of miles of lowland verges in England turn white with drifts of cow parsley **A** but, just as this begins to die down, the heavier, denser heads of hogweed **B** take their place and can last the summer. In the north, especially in the hills, cow parsley is replaced by sweet cicely **C**, distinguished by the delicious aniseed smell of its leaves, often blotched with white, and its fruits up to 2cm long.

If the verges are cut but the hedge bottom is left, another umbel becomes obvious in June and July, rough chervil **F**, recognisable by its purple spotted, hairy stems. This in turn is succeeded by upright hedge-parsley **D**, with unspotted stems and bristles rather than hairs.

Verges kept short in mid summer, especially on chalk or limestone, often produce a crop of burnet-saxifrage **E** in

Parsley 3 cont.

August and September, recognised by its drooping, unopened flower heads.
A Cow parsley *Anthriscus sylvestris*. Masses of white flowers in spring gave rise to its other name, 'Queen Anne's lace'. Flowers April—June.
B Hogweed *Heracleum sphondylium*. Hairy leaves divided into simple, coarsely toothed leaflets; large, round fruits persist long into autumn. Flowers June—September.
C Sweet cicely *Myrrhis odorata*. Any part crushed between fingers smells of aniseed, stems softly hairy; fruits dark brown and shining when ripe. Flowers May—June.
D Upright hedge-parsley *Torilis japonica*. Last of common roadside 'umbels' to flower; stems rough with down-turned bristles; fruits spine-covered. Flowers July—August.
E Burnet-saxifrage *Pimpinella saxifraga*. Lower leaves simply lobed, upper leaves much divided; no bracts or bracteoles at base of lower or upper 'umbrellas'. Flowers July—September.
F Rough chervil *Chaerophyllum temulentum*. Flowers along roadsides after **A**. Stems hairy and purple spotted; leaves also hairy. Flowers June—July.

Identification table to sixteen common 'Umbels'

Strong smell: rub leaf between fingers and sniff.

Neither bracts nor bracteoles: no leaf-like appendages below upper or lower 'umbrella' stalks.

Bracts divided: leaf-like appendages below lower 'umbrella' stalks are toothed or divided into fine thread-like segments.

Leaves simply pinnate: main leaves only once divided into segments, which may be toothed or cut but never as far as their mid-rib.

Bracteoles only: no leaf-like appendages below lower 'umbrella' stalks.

Fruit round: looking at broadest side of fruit it is not more than one-and-a-half times as long as wide.

Key +present −absent ±sometimes

stems spotted	strong smell	flowers yellow	neither bracts nor bracteoles	bracts divided	stems solid not hollow	stems hairy	leaves simply pinnate	bracteoles only	fruit round	garden	roadside	waterside	
+	−	−	−	−	+	+	−	−	−	−	+	−	rough chervil
+	−	−	−	−	−	−	−	+	−	+	+	−	hemlock
−	+	−	−	−	+	+	−	+	−	−	+	−	sweet cicely
−	+	−	−	+	+	+	−	−	−	+	+	−	wild carrot
−	+	+	+	−	+	−	−	−	+	+	−	−	fennel
−	+	+	+	−	−	+	+	−	+	+	+	−	wild parsnip
−	−	−	+	−	±	+	±	−	+	−	+	−	burnet-saxifrage
−	−	−	+	−	−	±	−	−	−	+	−	−	ground-elder
−	−	−	+	−	−	+	−	−	+	−	−	+	lesser water-parsnip
−	−	−	±	−	−	−	−	−	−	−	−	+	hemlock water-dropwort
−	−	−	−	−	+	+	−	−	+	−	+	−	upright hedge-parsley
−	−	−	−	−	+	±	−	+	−	−	+	−	hogweed
−	−	−	−	−	+	−	+	−	−	−	+	−	cow parsley
−	−	−	−	−	+	+	+	+	−	−	−	+	fool's water-cress
−	−	−	−	−	−	+	+	−	−	−	−	+	wild angelica
−	−	−	−	−	−	−	+	+	+	−	−	−	fool's parsley

A

F

D

B

C

E

Mercuries and spurges

Spurges, like poppies, exude juice when the stem is broken. The white, milky latex becomes obvious when the stems of the two annual species, which invade our paths, flower beds and potato patches, aggravatingly snap off just above the ground during weeding. Both are yellowish-green and have roundish upper leaves, broadest near the tip. The smaller, appropriately named petty (*petit*) spurge **A** rarely exceeds 20cm and is specially at home on gravel paths. The larger sun spurge **B** is also well named; seen from above, it looks like a child's drawing of the sun.

Many gardens also have another spurge — the biennial caper spurge **C** — originally grown as a medicinal plant because the juice could be used as a laxative. It can become a weed though it may be treasured for its attractive blue-green coloration and rigid, upright stems with their stiffly held pairs of opposite leaves.

Dwarf spurge **D** is an annual similar to petty spurge but with narrow, pointed, green leaves. It is rare in gardens and confined to arable fields in south-east England. Wood spurge **E** is a tall perennial, common in old woodlands south of a line joining Norwich to Shrewsbury. It is the only hairy spurge native to Britain. Because of its size, it is the best species in which to study the curious apparent flowers of spurges, which are really clusters of separate male and female flowers, each consisting of a single stamen or a single ovary, surrounded by a cup of bracts bearing conspicuous glands.

The mercuries belong to the same family as the spurges, the Euphorbiaceae, but lack the milky juice. Like them, they have male and female flowers, but they are isolated on separate plants and are without those conspicuous glands. They have round bristly fruits, **Fa**, **Ga**.

Dog's mercury **F** is one of our commonest and drabbest woodland herbs — a perennial forming an almost continuous carpet of hairy, light-green leaves. Annual mercury **G** is a weed of gardens mainly south and east of a line joining the Wash to the Severn. Its leaves are bright green and hairless.

A Petty spurge *Euphorbia peplus*. Yellowish-green annual found on nearly every garden path; rounded, short-stalked leaves, more pointed near top of stem. Flowers April—November.

B Sun spurge *Euphorbia helioscopia*. Yellowish-green annual of cultivated ground; flowers surrounded by glands without horns. Flowers May—October.

C Caper spurge *Euphorbia lathyroides*. Bluish-green biennial cultivated for ornament but rare native of woods on limestone in southern England. Flowers June—July.

D Dwarf spurge *Euphorbia exigua*. Bluish-green annual with narrow, spirally arranged leaves. Flowers surrounded by moon-shaped glands with long, slender horns. Flowers June—October.

E Wood spurge *Euphorbia amygdaloides*. Perennial with hairy leaves and stems up to 1m high which are sterile in first year. Flowers March—May.

F Dog's mercury *Mercurialis perennis*. Conspicuous male flowers on long lateral spikes with yellowish-green stamens, females hidden among upper leaves. Flowers February—April.

G Annual mercury *Mercurialis annua*. Hairless annual with branched stems; male and female flowers usually on separate plants. Flowers July—October.

Knotweeds, knotgrasses and their relations

Knotweeds were introduced to British gardens for their decorative qualities but often have become pestilential weeds. Japanese knotweed **A**, introduced from Japan in 1825, is the biggest problem. Extensive underground creeping stems dominate river banks, etc., with canes 2m high.

Giant knotweed **B** is taller with canes up to 4m in height and has not been introduced so widely. The leaves are markedly heart-shaped. It was introduced from Japan before 1861. Knotgrass **C** is sure to be found among the potatoes. Procumbent where trodden upon, it may grow up to half a metre tall when sheltered; small, oval leaves arise from knotty swellings on the stem which give it its name. Small pink or white flowers occur in clusters of 1–6 where leaf and stem meet and develop 3-angled black nutlets.

Also among the vegetables you could find a weed with black nutlets but greenish flowers arranged in long loose spikes. This is black bindweed **D**, an annual easily recognised by its broad, heart-shaped leaves. A cornfield weed, the nutlets are harmful to farm animals.

Redshank **E** is another annual garden weed in the same family, but with red stems or 'shanks', dense clusters of usually pink, or white, flowers and narrow-pointed leaves, often with a large black blotch at the base.

Water-pepper **F** lives up to its name. Growing near water, especially where soils are acid, it resembles redshank but has greenish flowers and yellowish-green spotless leaves which, when nibbled, produce a strong peppery taste and a burning sensation. The acrid juice of the leaves can make the skin itch.

The clustered spikes of common bistort **G** are so attractive that a reddish form is frequently grown. In the Lake District the wild form was also 'cultivated' and the young leaves eaten.

Whereas the pink spikes of common bistort make a fine show on land, amphibious bistort **H** makes its best display floating on water. A remarkable plant, it has two forms: aquatic with hairless floating leaves and terrestrial with hairy leaves which have more rounded bases. Both may be found on a single plant.

A Japanese knotweed *Reynoutria japonica*. Whitish flowers and abruptly pointed leaves almost as broad as long. Flowers August—October.

B Giant knotweed *Reynoutria sachalinensis*. Flowers are greenish and heart-shaped leaves one-and-a-half times as long as broad. Flowers August—September.

C Knotgrass *Polygonum aviculare*. Leaves on main stem larger than those on flowering stems; nutlets are slightly longer than flower. Flowers May—October.

D Black bindweed *Polygonum convolvulus*. Only fruits are black: only bindweed which climbs clockwise. Flowers July—October.

E Redshank *Polygonum persicaria*. Abundant in well-manured fields, waste places and on pond margins.

F Water-pepper *Polygonum hydropiper*. Greenish or reddish flowers, covered in glandular dots, drooping heads. Flowers July—September.

G Common bistort *Polygonum bistorta*. *Bistorta* is from Latin *bis* meaning twice, and *tortus* (twisted) refers to contorted underground stems, hence snake-weed. Flowers June—August.

H Amphibious bistort *Polygonum amphibium*. Land and water forms so different difficult to accept as one species. Flowers July—September.

Docks and sorrels

There are two large common docks, which are up to 1m high, in gardens and on roadside verges. Broad-leaved dock **A** has leaves over 10cm wide with blunt tips. These are the leaves usually picked by children to remove the pain of nettle stings and which were used in former times to wrap butter. Curled dock **B** has long, narrow leaves with a pointed tip and a wavy margin. The two are closely related and hybrids are often found. Troublesome in gardens with their long, persistent roots.

Two other, smaller, docks usually less than 60cm high and closely resembling each other are found in roadside verges, river banks and on woodland rides. Both have oblong leaves decreasing in size up the plant, but in clustered dock **C** there are small leaves on the smallest flowering branches, whereas in the wood dock **D** these upper branches are leafless. These plants can be identified at a distance by the angle their flowering branches make with the main stem. If less than 30 degrees, it is wood dock; if between 30 and 90 degrees it is clustered dock.

The flowers and fruits of docks are very curious. The flowers consist of 2 whorls of 3 segments: the outer ones are always small and thin, but the inner ones become enlarged after pollination, surrounding a single triangular nut as it ripens, and may develop swellings or tubercles in the centre and characteristic marginal teeth.

Sorrels have leaves which are acid to the taste; the name comes from an old French word *surele* which means sour. Common sorrel **E** has long been prized as a vegetable used to flavour sauces. It is one of the most frequent plants of old grassland and may occur in a well-established lawn. If left unmown, it will grow 30—60cm tall, its stems and lance-shaped leaves turning a brilliant crimson when it bears fruit in autumn.

On dry, sandy lawns and on heathland sheep's sorrel **F** predominates. It is smaller, scarcely exceeding 30cm in height. The leaves are arrow-shaped with two lobes at the base which are pointed outwards.

Sorrels are unusual in having separate male and female plants which produce flowers of different sizes. Males are larger and more conspicuous, producing abundant pollen, blown by the wind to the female flowers. Flowers without scent or nectar.

A Broad-leaved dock *Rumex obtusifolius*. Leaves are about twice as long as broad with blunt tips and flat margins; fruits have toothed margins, one segment with roundish tubercle. Flowers June—October.

B Curled dock *Rumex crispus*. Largest leaves about five or six times as long as broad with pointed tips and undulating margins; fruits have toothless margins, 1–3 segments with oblong tubercle. Flowers June—October.

C Clustered dock *Rumex conglomeratus*. Dull green leaves have stalks as long as blade; flowering branches at over 30 degrees to stem; fruits have toothless margins, 3 segments with oblong tubercles. Flowers July—October.

D Wood dock *Rumex sanguineus*. Bright green leaves have stalks less than half as long as blade; flowering branches less than 30 degrees to stem; fruits have toothless margins, 1 segment with roundish tubercle. Flowers June—July.

E Common sorrel *Rumex acetosa*. Lance-shaped leaves have basal lobes pointing downwards; uppermost leaves clasp stem. Flowers May—June.

F Sheep's sorrel *Rumex acetosella*. Leaves arrow-shaped with basal lobes pointing outwards, uppermost leaves not clasping stem. Flowers May—August.

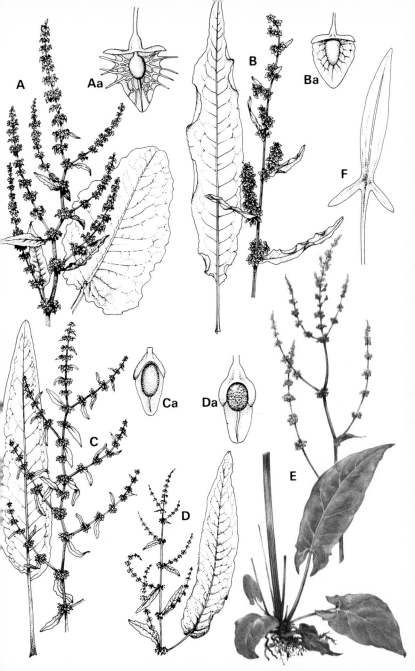

A

Aa

B

Ba

F

C

Ca

D

Da

E

Nettles and allies

Nettles are far too common to need introduction and so unpleasing to eye and body that they are often eradicated from the garden before their interest is appreciated.

Two stinging nettles are abundant and both have separate male and female plants **Da**. The flowers are green, lack separate sepals and petals and have parts arranged in fours.

Common nettle **D** is a perennial, native in woods and hedge banks but well adapted, by its tough, spreading, yellow roots, to invade waste ground and the untended garden. It should be tolerated in any garden in moderation: it is the favoured food plant of the caterpillars of peacock and small tortoiseshell butterflies which give delight outdoors in summer (and often indoors in winter); young shoots can be picked (with gloves), boiled and eaten (with butter) as a vegetable which tastes like spinach.

Annual nettle **E** is especially a weed of the potato patch, where the soil is regularly disturbed. It is easily pulled up but, beware, it also stings. It can be easily recognised even when young by its often yellowish leaves, which are only slightly longer than broad.

Two non-stinging members of the nettle family may also be found in walled gardens, both more conspicuous for their leaves than their flowers, which are green and unlovely. In pellitory-of-the-wall **A** the whole plant has a reddish tint, giving a warm glow to ruins in contrast to the bright yellow wallflowers so often nearby. Shade at the bottom of walls is the most likely place to find mind-your-own-business

C, especially in south and west Britain. Here almost unnoticed, it can speedily produce moss-like cushions of many small leaves which hide the solitary flowers.

Hops **B** need poles, not walls. Though a perennial, the stems are annual, often climbing over 6m carrying vine-like leaves high in the hedges by spiralling clockwise round their branches. Like nettle, it also has separate male and female plants but it is the flowers of the latter which produce the cones used in brewing beer.

A Pellitory-of-the-wall *Parietaria judaica*. Flowers of three kinds, male, female and hermaphrodite **Aa**; young stamens curved inwards spring outwards scattering pollen cloud if touched when ripe **Ab**. Flowers June—October.

B Hop *Humulus lupulus*. Native in wet woods by streams in southern half of Britain; elsewhere relic of cultivation by beer makers. Flowers July—August.

C Mind-your-own-business *Soleirolia soleirolii*. Introduced from Corsica and Sardinia as greenhouse plant for its bright green leaves; spreads rapidly, so also called 'mother-of-thousands'. Flowers May—October.

D Common nettle *Urtica dioica*. Lower leaves shorter than their stalks; fibre in stems once spun and used to make sheets and table cloths. Flowers June—August.

E Annual nettle *Urtica urens*. Lower leaves longer than their stalks; do not confuse with dead-nettles (page 84) with similar shaped leaves but much more conspicuous flowers. Flowers June—September.

A

Ab

Aa

B

C

Da

D

E

Heathers and bilberries

Heather gardening is only really possible if you live on sandy or peaty, acid soils, though the early-flowering alpine *Erica herbacea* will grow in lime-rich soils. However, heathers grow abundantly in the wild, particularly in the north and west of Britain. The commonest is the true heather or ling **A** absent from only a few areas where chalk and limestone dominate in central and eastern England. It is an invaluable plant to man and animals, being the main food of grouse, which eat the tender shoots produced after controlled rotational burning every ten to fifteen years, and also being used for thatching, bedding and fence repairs. The flowers are full of nectar and most attractive to bees which produce a dark honey from it.

Two other heathers are commonly found with ling, and can be distinguished from it by their flowers: in ling each flower has four separate petals and four coloured sepals which are longer than the petals **Aa**, whereas other heathers have sepals much shorter than the petals, which are joined to form a pendulous bell. Bell heather **B** has crimson-purple bells and hairless leaves in bunches of indefinite numbers. It is found in the drier parts of heaths and moors and can be abundant on coastal cliffs and inland rocks.

In contrast cross-leaved heather **C** is more frequent in wetter areas, notably in peat bogs; the bells are rose-pink and the hairy leaves form fours in a cross at each node.

The flowers of bilberry **D** are a clear indication that it also belongs to the heather family. They are flask-shaped with a long stigma surrounded by a ring of 10 stamens. One of our commonest upland shrubs, it is unusual in being deciduous. The bilberry is well-loved by summer visitors to the moors because of the blue-black edible berries which are ripe from July onwards and make excellent tarts and jams.

A Heather *Calluna vulgaris*. Tiny leaves in opposite pairs; 'lucky' white heather can be found in small quantity on most moors. Fruit capsule persistant **Ab**. Flowers July—September.

B Bell heather *Erica cinerea*. Leaves apparently in indefinite numbers in bunches at each node but actually in a whorl; flower crimson-purple, rarely white; capsule hairless. Flowers July—September.

C Cross-leaved heather *Erica tetralix*. Leaves in fours and with sepals covered in long glandular hairs; flowers rose-pink; capsule hairy. Flowers July—September.

D Bilberry *Vaccinium myrtillus*. Leaves bright green, and finely toothed; stems wiry and angled; fruits at first covered with a bloom like plums. Flowers April—June.

Primroses and gentians

Few plants can be more familiar than the primrose **H**. A clump of its beautiful butter-yellow flowers brightens most gardens. In the west of England it begins to flower soon after Christmas, hence 'primrose', the first rose of spring. It grows in woods and old grassland throughout Britain.

Cowslips **G** are also victims of the trowel but, being particularly plants of grassland, the major cause of their decline has been the plough, as old herb-rich meadows have been changed into crops of grass and clover. Cowslip is a polite form of 'cowslop' or cow-pat, because it grows in clumps.

There are two other common yellow-flowered members of the primrose family, one of which, creeping-jenny **D**, is often grown in rock gardens or hanging baskets. It is also known as moneywort or herb twopence because the leaves are shaped like old pennies on either side of the creeping stems. Yellow pimpernel **E** is very similar but the leaves, instead of being rounded, come to a point. It grows in damp woods and shady hedgerows almost everywhere but is rare in the driest part of eastern England and uncommon in gardens. In contrast scarlet pimpernel **F** appears in most kitchen gardens; it can be instantly recognised by its straggling habit, opposite pairs of shining, un-toothed, green leaves and the five-petalled scarlet (rarely blue) flowers; known as poor-man's weather-glass because flowers close before rain.

Members of the gentian family also have opposite pairs of leaves which alternate at right angles up the stem. In autumn gentian **C** they are pointed and close together, overlapping to produce a compact, pyramidal plant with a mass of 5-petalled, purple, star-like flowers. Common centaury **B** has more rounded leaves, some distance apart; flowers in compact, often flat-topped clusters.

Yellow-wort **A** can be instantly recognised not only by its yellow flowers of 6–8 petals but by the cabbage-coloured leaves which clasp each other round the stem. All three 'gentians' grow together in lime-rich grassland and sand dunes.

A Yellow-wort *Blackstonia perfoliata*. Stems branch regularly with a flower in angle of each pair; like other members of gentian family, whole plant is bitter to taste. Flowers June—October.

B Common centaury *Centaurium erythraea*. Annual with an overwintering rosette of spoon-shaped leaves; pointed petals connected to form long tube. Flowers June—October.

C Autumn gentian *Gentianella amarella*. Commonest gentian in south with parts arranged in fives, replaced in north on acid soils by field gentian with 4 sepals and petals. Flowers July—October.

D Creeping-jenny *Lysimachia nummularia*. Calyx of broad overlapping sepals; flowers 2–3cm across on stout stalks, shorter than leaves. Flowers June—August.

E Yellow pimpernel *Lysimachia nemorum*. Calyx of narrow, non-overlapping sepals; flowers about 1cm across on slender stalks longer than leaves. Flowers May—September.

F Scarlet pimpernel *Anagallis arvensis*. Flowers develop into globe-shaped capsules which split around equator; leaves stalkless, dotted with black glands beneath. Flowers June—August.

G Cowslip *Primula veris*. Leaves contract abruptly into stalk at base; flowers raised on strong stem, flower-stalks finely hairy. Flowers April—May.

H Primrose *Primula vulgaris*. Leaves taper gradually into stalk; flower-stalks shaggily hairy. Hybrid with cowslip has 'primrose' flowers raised on strong stem. Flowers January—May.

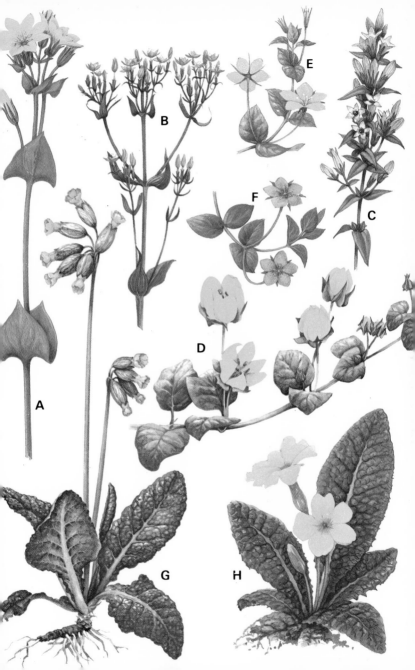

Borages and comfries

The borage family, which includes forget-me-nots, are often roughly hairy herbs with 5-lobed tubular or bell-shaped flowers arranged on stems which uncurl, as the flowers open, from the bottom upwards. Many were grown for their medical properties, hence *officinalis* in the scientific name (officina=drug-store).

Borage **A** is desirable in the herb garden: the young leaves have a faint, cucumber-like flavour which can garnish a salad and the flowers improve your claret cup. The brilliant blue, star-like flowers and greyish green leaves are often seen in summer in hedge banks near gardens, from which the plant has undoubtedly escaped.

Common comfrey **E** is also an invaluable herb. The leaves dipped in batter and fried are palatable, whilst the roots are full of mucilage, which has been used to treat sores, wounds and ulcers. The flowers vary in colour from pale yellow to carmine red. A vigorous hybrid was introduced from Russia and grown as a fodder plant: most roadside plants with purple or violet flowers are derived from this source.

The white-spotted leaves of lungwort **C** look so much like lungs that our ancestors supposed it was a sign that it would cure tubercular diseases. However, the plant is full of mucilage and its reputation as a cough medicine was probably soundly based. It escapes from gardens and is occasionally found in woods and thickets throughout lowland Britain.

The biennial viper's-bugloss **B** is one of our most beautiful wild flowers and would grace any garden, where it will attract attention not only from human visitors but from bees, butterflies and moths which feed on its sugary nectar. After pollination, each flower produces four nutlets said to resemble a viper's head. It is widespread on dry or sandy soils, especially dunes and sea cliffs.

The 4 nutlets of hound's-tongue **D** become covered with short, barbed spines very rough to touch **Da**. In contrast, the leaves are softly hairy and their shape and texture gave the plant its name. It grows on bare, dry soils such as sand dunes and lime quarries.

A Borage *Borago officinalis*. *Borago* may be derived from Latin word *burra*, a shaggy garment, referring to rough, hairy stem and leaves. Flowers June—August.

B Viper's-bugloss *Echium vulgare*. Upper lobes of funnel-shaped flowers longer than lower lobes; 4 of stamens visible, 1 hidden in the funnel. Flowers June—September.

C Lungwort *Pulmonaria officinalis*. Flowers at first pink but turn blue with age, hence several double names — Adam and Eve or Joseph and Mary (blue for a boy, pink for a girl?). Flowers March—May.

D Hound's-tongue *Cynoglossum officinale*. Leaves crushed between fingers give off strong smell of mice; horizontally spreading calyx exposes 4 bristly fruits. Flowers June—August.

E Common comfrey *Symphytum officinale*. Plant softly hairy with leaf blades running into wings down the stem. Hybrid Russian comfrey is rough to touch with no wings. Flowers May—September.

A

B

C

D

Da

E

Forget-me-nots

No garden would be complete without its border of forget-me-nots, difficult to be rid of as they seed profusely and germinate readily. Several species are cultivated or grow nearby in dry grassland or wet ditches. Often similar but can be distinguished by examination (with a hand-lens) and this identification table.

Take the table to the plant. Has it a calyx with hooked hairs sticking out at right angles? If 'yes', then it is one of the first four. Remove the corolla of a freshly opened flower (should come away in one piece); look sideways through the calyx teeth. Can you see the style? If so, it is longer than the calyx tube and your plant is either wood or changing forget-me-not. To distinguish between these two examine the flower-stalk. Is it shorter than or equal to the length of the calyx? If 'no', it must be wood forget-me-not **G**.

The commonest is field forget-me-not **A**, an annual of disturbed soils. The prettiest is changing forget-me-not **B**, another annual of arable fields, etc. Tiny flowers (2mm across) are yellow or white when open; later change to bright blue. When shedding seed, the flowering part of stem is no longer than the leafy part below. In contrast the seeding part of the similar early forget-me-not **C** is much longer than the leafy part: mainly on dry, shallow, sandy soils; flowers in April.

Common forget-me-nots of wet places are: water forget-me-not **D** on the margins of rivers, etc., and tufted forget-me-not **E** more frequent in marshes. A third, creeping forget-me-not **F**, grows on acid, peaty soils.

A Field forget-me-not *Myosotis arvensis*. Lobes of corolla concave, flowers under 4mm across **Aa**. Flowers April—September.

B Changing forget-me-not *Myosotis discolor*. Corolla tube twice as long as calyx; calyx teeth erect **Ba**; seeds dark brown. Flowers May—September.

C Early forget-me-not *Myosotis ramosissima*. Corolla tube shorter than calyx; calyx teeth spreading **Ca**; seeds pale brown. Flowers April—June.

D Water forget-me-not *Myosotis scorpioides*. Each tooth of calyx shaped like an equilateral triangle **Da**; hairs on stem sometimes erect. Flowers May—September.

E Tufted forget-me-not *Myosotis laxa*. Each tooth of calyx shaped like an isosceles triangle **Ea**; hairs on stem all laid flat. Flowers May—August.

F Creeping forget-me-not *Myosotis secunda*. Old flowers turned down; stems extremely hairy, hairs at right angles. Flowers May—August.

G Wood forget-me-not *Mysotis sylvatica*. Lobes of corolla flat, flowers 4–10mm across **Ga**. Flowers May—June.

Key +present −absent	calyx with hooked hairs	style longer than calyx tube	flower-stalk shorter than or equalling calyx	corolla more than 4mm across
wood f.	+	+	−	+
changing f.	+	+	+	−
early f.	+	−	+	−
field f.	+	−	−	−
water f.	−	+	−	+
creeping f.	−	−	−	+
tufted f.	−	−	−	−

Bindweeds and potatoes

Field bindweed **B** is far too common in most gardens and, once it invades the rock garden or the asparagus bed, is very difficult to eradicate. Its stout underground stems may go down almost 2m and any part broken off can form a new plant. Its saving grace is the handsome white or pinkish, trumpet-shaped flower which has a strong scent and is rich in nectar, making it attractive to many pollinating bees and flies.

Hedge bindweed **C** can raise its bell-like flowers 3m or more from the ground, twining its way through hedge or wire fence. The corolla of 5 joined petals varies in colour from white to bright pink with alternating white bands and is particularly attractive to bumble-bees and hover flies.

Our two bryonys are also hedge-climbers and both produce poisonous berries. White bryony **A** is the only native member of the cucumber family and climbs with the aid of tendrils. These are unusual because the spring-like coils which draw the plant to the hedge change direction in the middle of the tendril. Below ground is a massive, yellowish rootstock, once sold as a substitute for mandrake, a herb prized for its medicinal properties.

Black bryony **F** is not related to white bryony and is our only native member of the largely tropical yam family. Like the yam, it has a large (black) underground tuber, from which fresh stems arise in spring. These lack tendrils but climb by twining like a runner-bean.

Underground tubers and poisonous berries are also characteristic of the potato family. The commonest wild member, which often climbs high in hedges and wet woods, is bittersweet **D** but it may also be found lying flat over the pebbles of a shingly shore.

Though variable in habitat, the red berries and the flowers, with their 5 rich blue petals and central core of yellow anthers, are unmistakeable.

Black nightshade **E** is much more potato-like and often grows between their rows. It is an annual weed with small white flowers and green or black berries, difficult to take out by hand as the stem breaks at ground level when pulled.

A White bryony *Bryonia dioica*. Separate male and female plants (dioecious) **Aa**: male flowers 3–8 together on long stalks, female 2–5 together in short-stalked clusters. Flowers May—September.

B Field bindweed *Convolvulus arvensis*. Corolla up to 2–3cm across, surrounded at base by 5 small, blunt-pointed sepals. Flowers June—September.

C Hedge bindweed *Calystegia sepium*. Corolla 5–7·5cm across, surrounded at base by 5 acute-pointed sepals which are partially hidden by 2 leaf-like bracts. Flowers July—September.

D Bittersweet *Solanum dulcamara*. Young stems were once collected in autumn and dried for medicinal use; they taste bitter at first but become sweet with age. Flowers June—September.

E Black nightshade *Solanum nigrum*. Most plants have young green berries, turning black when ripe, but yellow berried plants occur rarely. Flowers July—September.

F Black bryony *Tamus communis*. Dioecious like white bryony; green flowers bell-shaped, male with 6 stamens as long as petaloid segments, reduced to knobs in female. Flowers May—July.

A

Aa ♂ ♀

B

C

D

E

F

Foxgloves and toadflaxes

The foxglove family produces a wide array of favourite garden flowers including, in addition to foxglove itself, snapdragons, speedwells, mulleins, monkey flowers and the genera *Hebe*, *Calceolaria*, *Penstemon* and *Nemesia*. Many of these species, originally introduced for garden ornament from other parts of the world, have subsequently escaped and become features of the countryside.

Snapdragon **A**, a native of the Mediterranean area, is well established on the walls of ruined abbeys and castles throughout England and, rarely, elsewhere. These 'wild' forms are usually reddish purple, though yellow, orange and white occur in garden beds. The mouth of the flower is closed by a bearded projecting platform which helps make it look like an animal's face or a mask, hence the Latin name *antirrhinum* meaning snout-like. Ivy-leaved toadflax **B** is another Mediterranean species which grows on walls; introduced early in the seventeenth century, it soon escaped and is now found throughout Britain, except in the north of Scotland. It has light, flat seeds which are easily blown by the wind and caught in crevices.

Monkeyflower **D** has come from even further afield; a native of western North America, it was first noted as an escape in 1830 but is now so well established it behaves like a native species, forming golden strips along streams in the north and west of Britain.

Common toadflax **C** is a small wild plant which could command a place in any garden with its striking spikes of yellow and orange snapdragon-like flowers. Each flower has a spur containing nectar which can only be reached by long-tongued bees which incidentally pollinate them whilst they feed.

Foxglove **E** has also been grown in gardens, where it can spread rapidly. The many very small seeds enclosed in the capsule which follows the glove-finger shaped flowers are easily scattered by the swaying stems in autumn winds. The drug digitalis is prepared from the dried, powdered leaves and is used to treat heart disease.

A Snapdragon *Antirrhinum majus*. Once supposed to possess supernatural powers and able to destroy spells: a garland round neck gave protection from witches (and dragons?). Flowers July—September.

B Ivy-leaved toadflax *Cymbalaria muralis*. Easily recognised by ivy-shaped leaves and snapdragon-like white and lilac flowers; spread by long, rooting runners. Flowers May—September.

C Common toadflax *Linaria vulgaris*. Growing in flax with upright stems and having narrow leaves like the crop gave toadflax its name; now mainly on roadsides and railway banks. Flowers July—October.

D Monkeyflower *Mimulus guttatus*. Pollinated by bees which touch the 2-lobed stigma on entry: lobes close together and insect then makes contact with anthers behind. Flowers July—September.

E Foxglove *Digitalis purpurea*. Flowers at base of stem open earliest, first in male stage, later female; bees working upwards bring pollen from male, upper flowers of one plant and deposit on female, lower flowers of another. Flowers May—September.

Speedwells 1

Twenty species of speedwell grow wild in Britain and seven or eight may be found in your garden. They are small herbs with opposite, generally rounded and uncut leaves and 4-petalled white, pink or blue flowers. The petals are flat and joined and distinctly marked with lines.

The majority of garden speedwells are annuals. The commonest and earliest to flower is the shiny-green leaved, bright-blue flowered, common field-speedwell **C**. It was introduced into this country in 1825 and now occurs everywhere; it is almost certain to be amongst the vegetables flowering in any month. Green field-speedwell **A** has light green leaves and, often, almost white flowers. Once a widespread arable weed it is now found more frequently in old gardens than elsewhere, equally at home on gravel paths or in herbaceous borders. Grey field-speedwell **E** has blue flowers, more dusty looking hairier leaves and may still be found in arable fields especially on lime-rich soils in the southern half of Britain. Also with grey leaves, but each with 3–7 lobes or teeth, is ivy-leaved speedwell **G**: recognised also by its Cambridge-blue flowers and hairy heart-shaped sepals. It is a spring flowering species which dies down in summer. The other common garden annual is wall speedwell **F**. The most upright of the species, it may consist of a single stem in dry places on walls and rock gardens, but can persist in well-cut lawns as well as forming large branching plants amongst the vegetables. Distinguished from the other annuals because flower stalks are shorter than the calyx.

Two perennials may invade your lawn where they will be almost impossible to eradicate — so enjoy a blue lawn. Thyme-leaved speedwell **D**, as the name suggests, has small rounded almost toothless leaves, which are

devoid of hairs. In contrast slender speedwell **B** has very hairy kidney-shaped leaves with much indented margins. Originally introduced from the Caucasus as a rock garden plant, the latter has now spread to grassland throughout the country.

A Green field-speedwell *Veronica agrestis*. Two halves of fruit parallel and rounded, covered in one kind of hair which is glandular-tipped, at least lower petal white. Flowers all year round.

B Slender speedwell *Veronica filiformis*. Flowering stalks thread-like, much longer than leaf stalks; hardly ever produces ripe seed, but spread by 'cuttings' attached to borrowed mowers. Flowers April—June.

C Common field-speedwell *Veronica persica*. Two halves of fruit diverge from base and are sharply keeled, covered in one kind of hair which is long but not glandular. Flowers all year round.

D Thyme-leaved speedwell *Veronica serpyllifolia*. Small upper leaves (bracts) with flower-stalks at base no longer than white or pale blue flowers. Flowers March—October.

E Grey field-speedwell *Veronica polita*. Two halves of fruit parallel and rounded covered in two kinds of hair — long gland-tipped and short hooked; all petals blue. Flowers all year round.

F Wall speedwell *Veronica arvensis*. Small upper leaves (bracts) narrow, untoothed, longer than flowers; calyx lobes similar, but smaller. Flowers March—October.

G Ivy-leaved speedwell *Veronica hederifolia*. Two forms occur: subsp. *lucorum* — middle lobe of leaf longer than wide, flower stalks 4–7 times length of calyx; subsp. *hederifolia* middle lobe wider than long, flower stalks 3–4 times length of calyx. Flowers March—May.

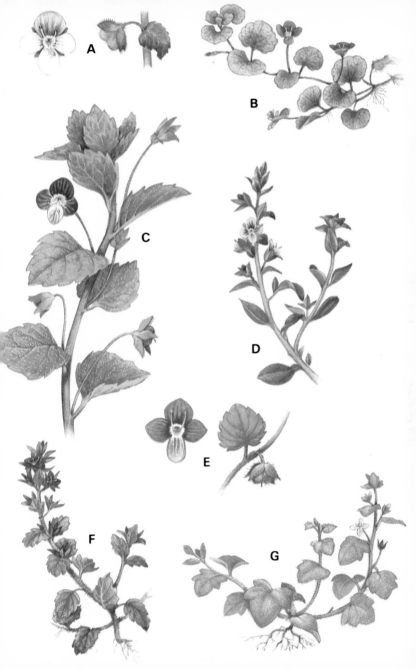

Speedwells 2

This group of speedwells is distinguished from all those on pp. 74-5, because in place of a single flower at the base of a small leaf there is a many-flowered stalk (raceme).

They are all perennials, and three are plants of relatively dry places with hairy leaves and stems. Germander speedwell **D**, is common in gardens or in nearby hedge banks and copses. The bright blue flowers have a white centre, hence another name, 'bird's-eye'. The two lines of hairs down the stem **Db** distinguish it from all other speedwells, and particularly from the very similar wood speedwell **E** which has hairs all round the stem **Ea**. As the name suggests this occurs in woods, and especially where these are damp in the south and west of Britain. The other hairy species is heath speedwell **F**. This grows in dry places, especially where the soil is free of lime, not only on heaths but in dry grassland and open woods. The individual pale blue flowers are attached by very short stalks to the upright flowering stem.

The remaining three species all occur in or near water and have hairless (glabrous) leaves and stems. The easiest to recognise is brooklime **A** with its creeping stems, shining, round stalked fleshy leaves, and racemes of bright blue flowers in pairs from opposite leaves. It occurs everywhere in wet muddy places by streams, and in ditches and at the edge of ponds. The flowers open in the sun, but half close in bad weather when the anthers touch the stigmas and self-pollination occurs.

The other two aquatic species have narrow, pointed leaves, without stalks, and are upright plants. Blue water-speedwell **B** has blue flowers whereas in the very similar pink water-speedwell **C** they are a much paler pink **Ca**. Both occur in ponds, streams and other wet places mainly in the lowlands of south and east Britain.

A Brooklime *Veronica beccabunga*. Once used in salads: the young leaves are not unpleasant (though rather bitter) and were said to cure scurvy. Flowers May—September.

B Blue water-speedwell *Veronica anagallis-aquatica*. When flowering stalks bear fruit they are held at 45° to the main stem; pollinated by flies. Flowers June—August.

C Pink water-speedwell *Veronica catenata*. Flowering stalks in fruit at right angles to the main stem; often hybridises with **B** to produce sterile intermediates. Flowers June—August.

D Germander speedwell *Veronica chamaedrys*. Leaves very shortly stalked; ripe capsules hidden by longer sepals **Da**; stems with two lines of hairs **Db**. Flowers March—July.

E Wood speedwell *Veronica montana*. Similar to Germander speedwell, but leaves on stalks up to 1cm; ripe capsules prominent, twice as long as sepals; stems hairy all round **Ea**. Flowers April—July.

F Heath speedwell *Veronica officinalis*. Leaves greyish, hairy on both sides: flower spikes dense, pyramid-shaped; dried flowers used as a mild diuretic. Flowers May—August.

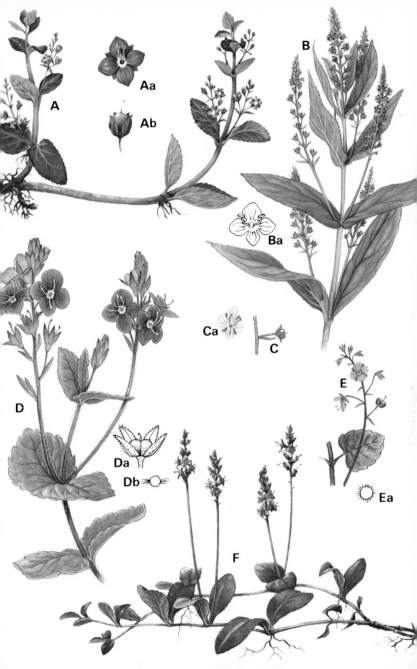

A

Aa

Ab

B

Ba

Ca

C

D

Da

Db

E

Ea

F

Louseworts and rattles

This colourful collection of wild flowers all belong to a section of the Foxglove family which has spikes of 2-lipped flowers which develop inflated capsules. In addition they are all partial parasites: although they have green leaves and normal roots they may grow only poorly unless these roots can fix onto those of neighbouring herbs in the grassland or woodland they inhabit.

Eyebright **A** is an annual which often grows in thousands on heaths and in short grassland, especially near the sea where it parasitises plantains and clovers. There are many different forms varying in flower colour from white to violet, and in degrees of branching and hairiness.

Common cow-wheat **B** is a yellow-flowered annual which occurs in large colonies on heaths, moors and, most frequently in dry sunlit woods. The scientific name *Melampyrum* and the English name both refer to the seeds which look like blackened grains of wheat.

Yellow rattle **F** also occurs in thousands in old meadows and marshes. The handsome yellow, hooded flowers with violet lower lip develop into swollen capsules containing numerous large, flat, kidney-shaped seeds which rattle in the wind when dry.

Red rattle is another name for the annual marsh lousewort **D** which refers not only to the pinkish-purple flowers, but also to the whole plant which has stems and much divided leaves suffused with purple. Its 'rattle' (the swollen calyx) is hairy **Da**.

In contrast the perennial common lousewort **E** has smooth capsules **Ea** and the plant is a much paler purple.

Louseworts were so named because they grow in marshes and wet meadows where sheep become infected with lice or liver flukes.

Red bartsia **C** is also tinged with purple, but is easily recognised by its undivided leaves and by the small pink flowers arranged on one side of their spikes only. Abundant in arable fields and open disturbed grassland throughout Britain.

A Eyebright *Euphrasia officinalis*. Stalkless leaves arranged in alternating pairs, overlapping in short, un-branched, coastal forms; capsule hairy often hidden by leafy bracts. Flowers June—September.

B Common cow-wheat *Melampyrum pratense*. Flowers 1–3cm long in pairs all pointing in one direction; corolla tube much longer than calyx. Flowers May—October.

C Red bartsia *Odontites verna*. Northern plants have branches at 45° and flowers shorter than bracts; southern plants have branches at wide angle and flowers longer than bracts. Flowers June—August.

D Marsh lousewort *Pedicularis palustris*. Upper lip of corolla with 4 teeth; erect annual of wet places often in standing water. Flowers May—September.

E Lousewort *Pedicularis sylvatica*. Upper lip of corolla with 2 teeth; prostrate perennial of damp heaths and acid grassland. Flowers April—July.

F Yellow rattle *Rhinanthus minor*. Dry meadow forms have broad leaves and branches from first ot second pair below flowers; forms in marshes are narrower-leaved and branch lower. Flowers May—August.

Mints

Nearly everyone with a garden has a patch of mint, usually within easy reach of the back door. Mints have a wide range of culinary uses — jelly, juleps and salads are all to be recommended, while mint tea is a refreshing beverage and a cure for indigestion.

The commonest mint in gardens is spearmint **A**, which has narrow, pointed, hairless leaves with numerous prominent teeth along the margins. Another kind, which is frequently found in cottage gardens, is the more delicately flavoured apple mint **B** with broad, rounded hairy leaves with inconspicuous teeth. A third mint, which is less frequently cultivated, but cannot be mistaken because of its pungent and familiar smell, is peppermint **C**: the whole plant is reddish-purple and the leaves, though pointed, are broader than spearmint's.

Many cultivated mints, including peppermint and apple mint, are sterile hybrids which rarely produce any fertile seeds, but send out long rooting runners. So when we need a new mint we do not purchase a packet of seeds, but we buy it as a plant or beg a rooted cutting from a neighbour. By this means 'clones' have been spread throughout Britain — all really coming from one original parent plant.

So vigorous are these hybrid mints that they produce far more leaves than even the most mint-conscious cook can consume and the surplus have to be dug up and committed to the dump. From here many of them have 'escaped', creeping into roadside hedges or down into deep ditches to add colour and scent to the countryside. Peppermint in particular can form brilliant purple patches along marshy stream banks. Here it may mingle with one of the two widespread wild mints which grow in Britain — water mint **D**. This too has a most pungent smell and is one of the parents of the hybrid peppermint, the other being the spearmint.

Water mint has rounder leaves than peppermint and the flowers, instead of forming a long spike, are arranged in whorls with the largest forming a pompom' at the top. In contrast, the other common wild mint, corn mint **E**, has no 'pom-pom' at the top of the stem, just a tuft of oval, pointed leaves which, when rubbed in the fingers, do not give off the familiar scent of mint.

A Spearmint *Mentha spicata*. Stems end in a long 'spike' of adjacent whorls at flowering in August—September.

B Apple mint *Mentha x villosa*. A hybrid of which spearmint is one of the parents and the rare round-leaved mint the other. As with all hybrid mints, the stamens are shorter than the bell-shaped flower. Flowers August—September.

C Peppermint *Mentha x piperita*. A hybrid which derives spike of flowers from spearmint and purple coloration from water mint. Sepals and flowerstalks are hairless. Flowers July—October.

D Water mint *Mentha aquatica*. Crushed underfoot perfumes a marshland walk; stems and leaves not obviously hairy. Flowers July—October.

E Corn mint *Mentha arvensis*. A weed of arable fields and woodland rides, has obviously hairy stems and leaves. Flowers May—October.

Marjoram and thyme

All these members of the mint family have the square stems, opposite pairs of undivided leaves at right angles to each other, and 2-lipped 4-stamened flowers which are its visual diagnostic features. In addition, and most importantly, the plants are often covered in glandular hairs which produce an aromatic fragrance when rubbed between the fingers or put into the cooking pot. Others are attractive and grown for ornament so that most are familiar garden plants.

Garden thyme is an upright woody plant, 30–47cm high, which comes from the Mediterranean and does not grow wild in Britain. Our wild thyme **E** has long creeping branches forming dense mats in dry grassland, in sand dunes and on rocky mountain ledges.

The marjoram grown in the herb garden may also be a Mediterranean species, but wild marjoram **C** contains a pungent oil once sold in shops as 'Oil of Thyme' so should not be spurned. It occurs in dry and usually lime-rich grassland and hedgebanks throughout lowland Britain.

Wild basil **B** lacks the strong aroma of marjoram so is rarely grown in gardens, but may be found with it in the wild on dry, lime-rich soils in hedge banks, woodland borders and scrub. It is a much hairier plant than marjoram which gives its leaves a dull (not shining) appearance.

Selfheal **D** was once prized as a cure for sore throats and given the scientific name *brunella*, the medical name for that infection. However neither this property nor that of healing could be relied upon. It can, however, be relied upon to occur in grassland throughout Britain where its spreading stems produce large circular patches.

Bugle **A** has a superficial similarity to selfheal but the individual flowers are quite different: it has virtually no upper lip to the corolla whereas selfheal has an obvious hood hiding the anthers. The short, stiff, upright, purple stems of bugle colour the floor of damp woods and meadows everywhere in May and June.

A Bugle *Ajuga reptans*. Upper lip of corolla reduced to 2 short teeth; outer pair of stamens obviously shorter than the inner. Flowers May—July.

B Wild basil *Clinopodium vulgare*. Four stamens of similar length clustered under upper lip of corolla **Ba**; all flowers male and female (hermaphrodite); flowering stems little branched above. Flowers July—September.

C Marjoram *Origanum vulgare*. Longer pair of 4 stamens, longer than upper lip of corolla **Ca**; some flowers hermaphrodite, others, smaller are female only; flowering stems branched above. Flowers July—September.

D Selfheal *Prunella vulgaris*. Outer pair of stamens longer than inner, hidden under hooded upper lip; bell-shaped calyx closes its mouth in fruit. Flowers June—September.

E Wild thyme *Thymus praecox*. Tiny 2-lipped flowers attract honey bees; some flowers hermaphrodite, others female only; when there are stamens they are longer than the upper lip. Flowers May—August.

A

B

Ba

C

Ca

D

E

Dead-nettles and hemp-nettles

Dead-nettles were so called because, though they have square stems and coarsely toothed leaves in opposite pairs like nettle, they do not sting.

Most large gardens can claim three species as weeds. The most persistent is the perennial white dead-nettle **C** which spreads by creeping underground stems and becomes enmeshed with garden plants in the herbaceous border. However a small patch may be tolerated for the large white hooded flowers suffused with green which are most attractive to long-tongued bees and appear throughout the year.

Red dead-nettle **D** is an annual and more easily controlled when it comes up amongst the sprouts in the kitchen garden. The pinkish-purple flowers are neither so handsome nor so large as the white dead-nettle's.

Henbit dead-nettle **F** is also annual and particularly frequent in dry, sandy gardens and in arable fields in the east of Britain. Easily recognisable by its stalkless pairs of leaves which appear to encircle the stem.

Common hemp-nettle **A** has flowers which resemble the dead-nettle's except that the lower lip has well developed lateral lobes. It can be recognised even without flowers by the stems which are markedly swollen below each pair of leaves and covered in downwardly directed hairs.

The lower lip of the flowers of yellow archangel **B** also have conspicuous lateral lobes. It is strikingly beautiful with dark, shining pointed leaves forming sheets of colour in open woods on heavy soils in spring, and spreading by long leafy runners.

Wood sage **G** is more frequent in dry, somewhat acid woods and heaths. Readily recognised by its spikes of yellow-green flowers and the hairy leaves with a surface wrinkled like a button-back chair.

Yellowish green is the characteristic colour of the leaves of gipsywort **E**, which are jagged, with large acute teeth, and often segmented below. However the flowers are white with 4 equal petals like mint and with only 2 stamens which are longer than the corolla tube (exserted). A frequent plant of marshes, and river banks.

A Common hemp-nettle *Galeopsis tetrahit*. Flowers variable in colour, pink, purple or white; calyx in fruit of 5 equal segments with long prickle-like points as long as calyx tube. Flowers July—September.

B Yellow archangel *Lamiastrum galeobdolon*. Galeobdolon is a combination of two Greek words for weasel and stench in reference to the nasty smell given off when the plant is rubbed between the fingers. Flowers May—June.

C White dead-nettle *Lamium album*. Common outside gardens in hedge banks, on roadsides and in waste places, but much rarer in the west where often only near railways. Flowers all year round.

D Red dead-nettle *Lamium purpureum*. Leaf margin with rounded teeth; corolla tube with a prominent ring of hairs hidden inside towards the base. Flowers March—October.

E Gipsywort *Lycopus europaeus*. Both hermaphrodite and female flowers occur; produces strong black dye, formerly used by gypsies to make themselves more like dark-skinned visitors from Egypt. Flowers June—Sept.

F Henbit dead-nettle *Lamium amplexicaule*. Lower leaves stalked, upper leaves sessile; the wavy margins are said to look as if bitten by hens. Flowers April—August.

G Wood sage *Teucrium scorodonia*. Once used to make beer bitter and for an anti-rheumatic tea. Flowers July—September.

Horehounds, skullcaps and woundworts

These last six members of the mint family are infrequently found in gardens. However black horehound **A** seems to wait at the garden gate hoping to be admitted, but this dusty-looking perennial of hedgerows and town roadsides rarely is, for it gives off a highly offensive smell noticed as soon as the leaves are crushed between the fingers. The scientific name *Ballota* comes from the greek, *ballo*, to reject.

The leaves of hedge woundwort **F** give off an equally offensive smell when crushed, but their hairiness and heart-shape make it easy to identify without risking unpleasantness. It is common in hedge banks and woodland margins throughout the lowlands.

Marsh woundwort **E** is similar, but has much narrower leaves, over four times as long as broad, and is usually found in marshes and on ditch and stream banks: in the west of Britain and in Ireland it can even be an arable weed.

Betony **D** is superficially similar, but is readily recognisable by its narrow heart-shaped leaves with rounded tips and very crinkly margins. A common plant of hedge bank, heath and open woodland once treasured as a herb; dried leaves produce a bitter herbal tea and, when powdered, a sort of snuff.

The same bitter flavour was a reason for ground-ivy **B** finding favour. Before the introduction of hops it was used in brewing to clear the beer and improve the taste and gained another name, alehoof. Its other name is misleading as it is neither related to nor looks like ivy, though it may grow with it in hedge bottoms.

Skullcap **C** is an unusual member of the mint family in that the deep blue flowers are in pairs, each pair facing the same way, as in cow-wheat. It grows in damp places like overgrown riverside meadows, streambanks or pond margins.

A Black horehound *Ballota nigra*. Course round-toothed leaves are similarly shaped at stem bottom and top; calyx like a funnel with its mouth guarded by 5 spiny teeth. Flowers June—October.

B Ground-ivy *Glechoma hederacea*. With its heart-shaped leaves and clusters of bluish flowers blooming in spring it might be mistaken for violets, but has opposite leaves and spreads by long-runners. Flowers March—May.

C Skullcap *Scutellaria galericulata*. Distinguished from other 'mints' by the 2-lipped corolla and calyx; the latter has a large leafy outgrowth on the back resembling a Roman helmet or *galerum* **Ca**. Flowers June—September.

D Betony *Stachys officinalis*. Most leaves long-stalked forming a basal rosette; corolla tube with scattered hairs inside, generally hairy outside. Flowers June—September.

E Marsh woundwort *Stachys palustris*. Leaf stalks very short (up to 6mm) or absent; flowers dull purple, corolla tube with few hairs inside except for a ring near the base. Flowers July—September.

F Hedge woundwort *Stachys sylvatica*. Leaf stalks long (up to 8cm); flowers claret-coloured, corolla tube with ring of hairs near base. Flowers July—August.

A

B

C

Ca

D

E

F

Plantains

Plantains have a rosette of leaves from the centre of which several cylindrical leafless stalks arise in summer, bearing long spikes of usually greenish or brownish flowers.

Five species occur in Britain, two of which are found in nearly every garden. In the lawn look for ribwort plantain **A** with strongly ribbed long, narrow leaves. On paths and in gateways and anywhere that is heavily trodden, you will find the big, broad, almost hairless leaves of greater plantain **B** pressed closely to the ground.

Less commonly, and only on lime-rich soils, the broad-leaved plantain — hoary plantain **C** — occurs. It is readily distinguished from greater plantain because its leaves are covered with white hairs and, when it flowers, by its purple and lilac stamens.

The other two species are most frequent near the sea, though they occur inland occasionally. Buck's-horn plantain **D** grows on sand and in rocks, and has toothed leaves whereas sea plantain **E** is found in saltmarshes and on exposed salt-sprayed cliffs and has narrow, fleshy leaves.

A Ribwort plantain *Plantago lanceolata*. Widespread in grassland, varying in size from 2·5–4·5cm: small forms occur in dry grassland, largest in lush meadows. Flowers have 4 white sepals and 4 brown petals. Flowers April—May.

B Greater plantain *Plantago major*. Seeds become sticky when wet and are carried in mud on boots and tyres. Spread to North America and Australasia where it is known as Englishman's-foot, for where the English trod the plantain followed. Flowers May—September.

C Hoary plantain *Plantago media*. Flowers produce delicate scent attractive to bees by which it is pollinated — other four species are wind-pollinated. Flowers May—August.

D Buck's-horn plantain *Plantago coronopus*. Rosette resembles a star; leaves usually divided but even when strap-shaped they can be recognized by having only 1–3 veins and by being slightly hairy. Flowers May—July.

E Sea plantain *Plantago maritima*. Fleshy leaves all strap-shaped with 3–7 faint veins. Flowers June—August.

Bedstraws and cleavers

Bedstraws and cleavers belong to one of the largest flowering plant families, the Rubiaceae, which includes tropical woody species like coffee and quinine. In Britain the most familiar genus is *Galium* which includes all the plants on this page. They are instantly recognised by their 4-angled stems, whorls of, usually, narrow leaves and clusters of small flowers with 4 joined petals which produce a pair of round, joined fruits.

The commonest in gardens, hedgerows, waste places and copses is cleavers **B** a name which refers to the way it cleaves to the passer-by. Stems **Ba**, leaves and pepper-corn-sized fruits **Bb** all have hooked hairs which catch in clothing or animal's fur. 'Sticky billy', 'hug-me-close' and 'sweethearts' are local names reflecting this clinging quality.

Hedge-bedstraw **D** may grow with cleavers on roadsides throughout the lowlands, but is easily distinguished by the total absence of hooked hairs on stem, leaf or fruit **Da**; the stem is often much swollen beneath each whorl of leaves.

When hedgerows and roadsides are on heavy, lime-rich soils prominent clumps of crosswort **C** may be picked out by their yellowish-green leaves and flowers. Both could be the origin of its name: leaves are cross-like in fours, as are the flowers.

Old hedgerows and ancient woodlands on free-draining lime-rich soils may be carpetted with pure white drifts of woodruff **A** in late spring. Spreads by slender creeping underground stems which can make it a dangerous plant to have in the garden. Lady's bedstraw **G** would be safer and would persist without being troublesome in a lightly mown lawn. One of the commonest species of old grassland, the name is a contraction of 'Our Lady's Bedstraw' suggesting that the Virgin Mary gave birth to Jesus in a stable with only wild flowers for bedding.

On heaths, moors and in acid grassland the trailing heath bedstraw **F** is the frequent species whilst in marshes, ditches and by pond margins the more erect common marsh-bedstraw **E** is the species most likely to be found.

A Woodruff *Galium odoratum*. Produces the odour of new-mown hay when dried; pure white flowers develop into fruits covered in hooked black-tipped bristles **Aa**. Flowers May —June.

B Cleavers *Galium aparine*. Also known as goosegrass because it was chopped up and fed to newly hatched goslings. Flowers June—August.

C Crosswort *Galium cruciata*. Flowers of 2 kinds, the outer male and female, the inner male only which soon fall; strong smell of honey attracts pollinators. Flowers May—June.

D Hedge-bedstraw *Galium mollugo*. A weak, often trailing, plant up to more than a metre tall with spreading branches; the similar but rarer upright hedge-bedstraw (*G. album*) is a more slender erect plant with ascending branches. Flowers June—September.

E Common marsh-bedstraw *Galium palustre*. Leaves 10–15cm in a whorl; broadest about the middle, blunt or acute but not ending in a fine point or mucro **Ea**. Flowers June—August.

F Heath bedstraw *Galium saxatile*. Leaves 6–8 in a whorl, broadest near the top, obtuse and ending in a distinct mucro **Fa**. Flowers June—August.

G Lady's bedstraw *Galium verum*. Leaves 8–12 in a whorl, narrow, tapering gradually to the point; smelling of new mown hay would make fragrant bedding. Flowers July—August.

Aa

A

Ba

B

Bb

C

D

Da

E

Ea

F

Fa

G

Teasels and valerians

Teasels and valerians are a group with red-tinted flowers in compact heads which are familiar in the herbaceous border, the kitchen garden or the flower arrangement.

Teasel **A** is by far the most prominent and persistent. Instantly recognised by the egg-shaped spiny heads surrounded by many narrow-toothed bracts, and the opposite pairs of saw-edged leaves which join at the base to form a water-catching cup. This cup acts as a vegetable insect trap preventing predators from climbing higher. Fullers' teasel, used to tease cloth by the woollen industry, is a subspecies with cylindrical heads and stiffer down-curved spines. It is a native of southern Europe and still grown commercially in south Somerset.

Valerians are fragrant herbs with funnel-shaped flowers which develop into single fruits crowned with a ring or a tuft of hairs derived from the calyx **Bb**. The most handsome is red valerian **B** which was introduced to gardens from southern Europe in the 16th century and has since been parachuted onto castle walls and into old quarries where the wind has carried its downy fruits. Red and white forms **Ba** occur in most parts of lowland Britain.

Common valerian **D** is the most widespread and also has wind-dispersed feathery fruits. It grows in rough grassland, in hedgebanks and beside streams throughout Britain. The roots can be dried and used to make valerian tea which is still drunk, particularly in Germany, to prevent hysteria.

Cornsalad **C** or 'lamb's-lettuce' is presumably attractive to lambs as well as to man. Seeds can be bought and sown in autumn to produce edible leaves in spring before the early lettuces to make an attractive, if somewhat insipid, salad. Gathered in flower it has a more fragrant flavour but if allowed to seed it may become a weed. Elsewhere it is a native of lowland Britain in cornfields, on railway banks, on rocks and in dunes.

A Teasel *Dipsacus fullonum*. Heads consist of several hundred 4-lobed tubular flowers arranged with mathematical accuracy which start to open in a band round the 'equator' and then work 'north' and 'south'. Flowers July—August.

B Red valerian *Centranthus ruber*. Leaves have a bitter taste, but if cut very young make a pleasant addition to a dull salad. Flowers June—August.

C Cornsalad *Valerianella locusta*. Each lilac 5-lobed flower produces a single quadrangular, hairy fruit **Ca**; once flowering is over this slender annual dies and disappears. Flowers April—June.

D Common valerian *Valeriana officinalis*. The short rootstock produces a rather unpleasant smell when dried, said to be attractive to cats; very variable in size and leaf shape. Flowers June—August.

A

B

Ba

Bb

C

Ca

D

Knapweeds and scabious

Two knapweeds are widespread in Britain and striking enough to be given a corner at least in the wild garden where they will attract the eye as well as numerous bees and butterflies. Common knapweed **A** grows in rough grassland and on roadsides where it is easily recognised by its hard, knob-like heads, which give it another name — 'hard heads'. The stem is hollow and swollen beneath the heads, which are made of many closely overlapping scales with a blackish, hemispherical 'comb' of teeth at the tip. The scales enclose many reddish-purple 'flowers' (florets) usually short and tubular but occasionally, especially in the West Country, with a row of larger florets round the outside.

Larger outer florets are a constant and distinctive feature of greater knapweed **B**: they are sterile, functioning to attract insect pollinators to the fertile florets in the centre, each of which produces a single fruit or achene. The deeply cut and irregularly lobed leaves are also distinctive.

There are also two common species of scabious in Britain. They are both perennials with slender stems terminating in button-like heads of flowers. Though superficially similar to knapweeds, which belong to the daisy family, scabious are closely related to teasel. There are two obvious differences: knapweeds have florets in which the anthers are joined to form a tube around the style and which are all enclosed by scales within the 'head' whereas scabious have 'free' anthers and the scales (bracts) merely form a platform on which the flowers are arranged.

Field scabious **C** is the taller of the two, often reaching about a metre; its upper leaves are divided and very hairy whilst the flowers are light-blue, though if they are touched by a lighted cigarette they change colour to a brilliant green.

Devil's-bit scabious **D** is shorter, usually under half a metre; all leaves are undivided, often purple-margined, and covered in short hairs flattened to their surface; the flowers are deep blue.

A Common knapweed *Centaurea nigra*. Very variable; in the north with short stems, conspicuously swollen beneath black bracted heads, in the south slender stems, little swollen beneath paler heads. Flowers June—September.

B Greater knapweed *Centaurea scabiosa*. Bracts beautifully marked with blackish-brown horseshoe-shaped comb around a green base; rough grassland on lime-rich soils. Flowers July—September.

C Field scabious *Knautia arvensis*. Originally thought to be a cure for scabies the juice was used to treat sores of all kinds; banks and dry grassland everywhere. Flowers July—September.

D Devil's-bit scabious *Succisa pratensis*. The root ends abruptly and was believed to have been bitten off by the Devil who was envious of its curative powers; marshes, wet meadows and damp woodland rides. Flowers June—October.

A

B

C

D

Thistles and burdocks

Few gardens are lucky enough to lack thistles. They can be recognised at all seasons by their prickly leaves, in summer by their heads of purplish flowers, and in autumn by thistle-down, which may fill the air with white fluff.

The commonest thistle in garden beds is creeping thistle **A** so called because it spreads by means of underground stems which are scattered further by digging. It has no rosette of leaves pressed closely to the ground.

Spear thistle **B** also occurs in gardens. It is a biennial and plants in good soil make large, handsome over-wintering rosettes of very spiny leaves. The flower heads are almost twice the size of those of creeping thistle.

Marsh thistle **C** also makes conspicuous purple-tinged rosettes of leaves often fringing wet hollows in cattle pastures and in marshes but also grows in clearings in wet woods where the erect stems can reach almost 2m and are topped by clusters of small heads less than 2cm across. The florets vary in colour from dark reddish-purple to almost white.

If you live on clayey soils, your roadside ditches may be backed by welted thistle **D**. Over 1m tall, it can be recognised by its groups of 3–5 small flower heads of creeping thistle size, and the long wings or welts which clothe the stem from top to bottom.

On dry, lime-rich soils you are more likely to see musk thistle **E** with big, solitary, cup-shaped flower heads on stalks free of spines.

Burdocks have prickly heads like thistles but the rest of the plant lacks spines and has rhubarb-sized leaves.

Lesser burdock **F** has smaller flower heads usually less than 2·5cm across including spines, carried on short stalks, and often purple tinted. Common throughout Britain, it may occur in shaded gardens.

Greater burdock **G** has large flower heads up to 4·5cm across, carried on long stalks up to 10cm long, and never tinged with purple. It is only common in the south and east, where it is often abundant on river banks.

A Creeping thistle *Cirsium arvense*. Flower heads surrounded by spine-tipped bracts closely pressed to head; stalks without spines. Flowers July—August.

B Spear thistle *Cirsium vulgare*. Flower heads surrounded by spine-tipped bracts which stick out; stalks have spiny wings. Flowers July—October.

C Marsh thistle *Cirsium palustre*. Flower heads small, and clustered at top of stems which have conspicuous, continuous, spiny wings. Flowers July—September.

D Welted thistle *Carduus acanthoides*. Spiny base of each leaf continues down stem as wing or welt. Flowers June—August.

E Musk thistle *Carduus nutans*. Large solitary flower heads are surrounded by spiny bracts, outer ones bent backwards. Flowers May—August.

F Lesser burdock *Arctium minus*. Lower leaves oval-oblong, leaf stalks hollow. Flowers July—September.

G Great burdock *Arctium lappa*. Lower leaves heart-shaped, leaf stalks solid. Flowers July—September.

Daisies: single yellow

This is a large group of plants which all appear very similar. But by looking at the way the flowers and the leaves are arranged you can begin to sort them out.

There are surely very few people who cannot recognise a dandelion **A** in bloom or by its single clock of little parachutes at the top of an unbranched stalk. It is typical of the daisy family in that each 'flower' is made up of up to 200 individual florets **Aa**, which consist of 5 petals fused to form a tube and coloured wing, and which later develop into a spiny, ribbed separate fruit with its own parachute **Ab**. Even when the dandelion is not in flower, or these have been cut off by the lawnmower, it may still be recognised by the rosette of leaves with sharp pointed lobes.

Three other yellow 'daisies' on unbranched stems may be found in or around the garden. Mouse-eared hawkweed **B** is a dwarf plant of short turf with creeping stems and elliptical leaves which lie flat on the ground; they are green with a few long, stiff hairs above, but in contrast are white and woolly on the underside. The flower heads also show a contrast in colour, bright yellow above but streaked with crimson beneath.

Colt's-foot **C** is one of the earliest spring flowers of verges and waste places, flowering before the true leaves appear. The flowering stem is clothed in much-reduced scale-like leaves. The true leaves have down on the underside, which was once scoured off and used for tinder. Their rounded yet angular shape gives the plant its name.

In contrast the leaves of goat's-beard **D** are long and narrow and so grass-like that they are easily overlooked on the roadside verges where they grow, unless they are in flower. But they flower only in the morning and by 1 pm (BST) they have closed for the day — hence the alternative English name, 'Jack-go-to-bed-at-noon'.

Another yellow daisy with distinctive leaves is rough hawkbit **E**; they are toothed, but never deeply divided and covered in forked hairs which can be seen clearly with a lens **Ea**.

A Dandelion *Taraxacum officinale*. Long, lettuce-like leaves in rosette with several long-stalked flower heads; stem and leaves exude white 'milk' when broken. Flowers March—October, especially May.

B Mouse-eared hawkweed *Hieracium pilosella*. Name refers to ancient belief that juice of plant strengthened vision of hawks. Flowers May—August.

C Colt's-foot *Tussilago farfara*. Flowers close at night or in cold weather; heads droop after pollination but become upright when fruits ripen. Flowers March—April.

D Goat's-beard *Tragopogon pratensis*. Name refers to long, silky parachute which appears after the flower reopens to expose ripe fruits. Flowers June—July.

E Rough hawkbit *Leontodon hispidus*. Solitary heads are held on long, hairy, leafless stems up to half a metre tall; a plant of rough grassland especially on lime-rich soils. Flowers June—September.

A

Aa Ab

B

D

Ea

E

C

Daisies: branched yellow

There are a large number of daisy-like flowers with yellow heads on branched stems which grow in or near the garden. The commonest include the six on this page and the three sow-thistles (page 102). These last can be distinguished by their thistle-like leaves which 'bleed' a white latex when the stems are broken. These characteristics are shared with prickly lettuce **C** which is however readily distinguished from all others by the way its upper leaves are held vertically when exposed to the sun with edges oriented north-south, and with spines on the midrib underneath. It often grows by motorways giving drivers a rough idea of the direction they are going.

Two branched yellow daisies can be recognised by their leafless stems which may however have small, scale-like bracts: the proper leaves are all at ground level forming rosettes flattened to the turf in which they grow. Autumn hawkbit **E** has dandelion-like leaves often cut to the midrib and, if the flower head is turned over, it can be seen that the outer florets are reddish on the back. Often turns roadsides a golden yellow in August and September as dandelion does in May. Cat's-ear **B** has leaves with wavy margins which are never cut to the midrib and has flowers with outer florets grey-violet or greenish beneath. They develop into parachutes of hairs which have many side branches like a feather which are absent in the dandelion.

Nipplewort **D** is given away by its lower leaves in which the terminal lobe is larger than the side lobes and by its small flower heads containing fewer than 20 florets, on upright branches, which do not produce parachutes.

Smooth hawk's-beard **A** also has small flower heads, less than 1cm across; these develop proper parachutes though they are almost hidden by clasping bracts.

Common fleabane **F** is the last to flower and the one most likely to occur in marshes and wet meadows where its undivided and wrinkled, woolly leaves are unmistakeable. When burnt its smoke was supposed to drive away fleas — hence its English name.

A Smooth hawk's-beard *Crepis capillaris*. Clasping bracts around florets are of two sizes; inner all equal and more than twice as long as few small unequal outer ones. Flowers June—September.

B Cat's-ear *Hypochoeris radicata*. Leaves covered with many stiff, unbranched hairs raised on pimples; grassland everywhere, especially when lime-free. Flowers June—September.

C Prickly lettuce *Lactuca serriola*. Leaves have bitter flavour very unlike garden lettuce; milky juice exuded by broken stems was used in Middle Ages to prepare a sleep-inducing drug. Flowers July—September.

D Nipplewort *Lapsana communis*. The buds have a nipple-like appearance; hence the plant was once recommended as a cure for sore nipples. Flowers July—September.

E Autumn hawkbit *Leontodon autumnalis*. Leaves hairless or with a few hairs not raised on pimples; flower heads close in rain. Flowers July—October.

F Common fleabane *Pulicaria dysenterica*. Flower heads of up to 600 separate florets, darkest in the centre; used as a cure for dysentery but of doubtful value. Flowers August—September.

Groundsels, ragworts and sow-thistles

All three sow-thistles are common weeds of garden, arable field and waste places. Not only do they have thistle-like leaves, and bleed white latex when the stems are broken, but also their yellow flowers produce distinctive flattened oval fruits (achenes).

Perennial sow-thistle **E** has large, dandelion-sized flowers which, with the stems below, are densely covered in yellow, sticky, glandular hairs. It can spread rapidly by underground stems. The other two species are annuals with smaller flowers; prickly sow-thistle **F** has shining, spiny, dark-green leaves, rounded at the base where they join the stem whereas smooth sow-thistle **G** has dull, spineless pale-green leaves which are pointed at the base. The origin of the name sow-thistle is obscure, but the reason may be because sows had an unfailing instinct that eating these plants would increase their flow of milk.

Groundsel **D** is another plant frequently fed to domestic animals. This little annual must be known to every gardener and, although a minor pest, has its uses particularly in winter for feeding rabbits or the 'budgie'. The heads of flowers are inconspicuous, without petals, but forms with petals do occur, especially in the west.

Sticky groundsel **C** always has obvious petals though these are turned back against the cone-shaped heads **Ca**. The whole plant is 'gluey' to the touch and the parachutes of other 'daisies' are often caught by them on the windswept railway tracks and sea shores where they grow.

Oxford ragwort **B** is the commonest yellow 'daisy' on railway lines. Not sticky to touch (almost hairless), this annual was introduced to Oxford from Italy in 1794, escaped onto nearby railway lines and has since been spread in the wake of trains to towns throughout the kingdom.

The native common ragwort **A** is a handsome perennial with ragged leaves (hence ragwort) and plates of many heads of yellow flowers. Far too common in some overgrazed pastures where its poisonous properties can be a danger to cattle, especially when dried in May.

A Common ragwort *Senecio jacobaea*. Bracts round flowers brown-tipped. Favourite food of the cinnabar moth; the black and yellow striped caterpillars may leave nothing but the stem uneaten. Flowers June—October.

B Oxford ragwort *Senecio squalidus*. Bracts round flowers black-tipped; earliest flowering and longest flowering of ragworts found in the wild. Flowers May—December.

C Sticky groundsel *Senecio viscosus*. Covering of glandular hairs gives whole plant a greyish hue and deposits foul smell on fingers when rubbed. Flowers July—September.

D Groundsel *Senecio vulgaris*. Heads develop parachutes of fine white hairs hence name *Senecio* from the Latin *senex*, old man, with a head of white hairs. Flowers all year round.

E Perennial sow-thistle *Sonchus arvensis*. Cornfield weed which also occurs in hedge banks and along drift lines of sandy shores and salt marshes. Flowers July—October.

F Prickly sow-thistle *Sonchus asper*. Fruits broadest near the top, always brown and lacking any transverse wrinkles; leaf bases rounded. Flowers June—August.

G Smooth sow-thistle *Sonchus oleraceus*. Fruits broadest near the base, yellow at first, brown later with obvious transverse wrinkles; leaf bases pointed. Flowers June—August.

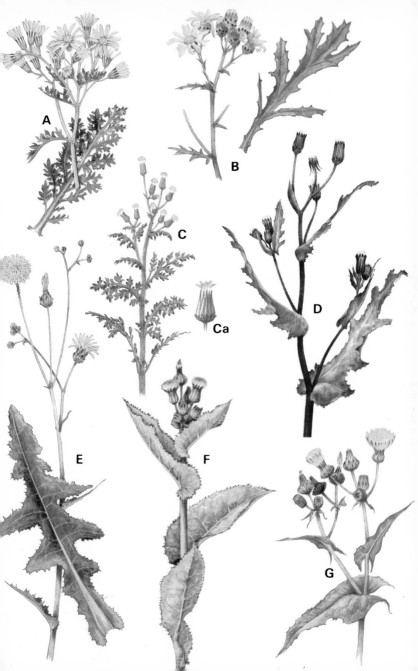

Ca

Daisies: single headed white

The beauty of the daisy **C** is often overlooked because it is so common: some gardeners regard it as a weed in the lawn but it can make a wonderful display in early summer. The display ceases in bad weather or after dark when the flowers fold their petals — the day's eye which is closed at night.

Few herbaceous garden borders are complete without the large white flowers up to 10cm across with yellow centres of the 'Shasta daisy'. Oxeye daisy **B** has heads only half the diameter, but makes a vivid impact where it forms sheets of white.

Feverfew **D** is another 'border' plant originally introduced from south-east Europe and cultivated for the drug it contains which brings down temperatures. It escapes onto nearby walls and into churchyards; its daisy-sized and daisy-like flowers and delicate green, divided leaves are unmistakeable.

Mayweeds and chamomiles are difficult plants for the farmer and the botanist. They are abundant in the farmer's crops and their finely divided leaves are resistant to weed killers: the botanist's problem is that several species look alike. The first rule of mayweed identification is smell it!

The easiest to identify is pineappleweed **E** or rayless mayweed. The flowers crushed between the fingers give off a distinct smell of pineapple, and the absence of white ray florets clinches the identification.

Scentless mayweed **G** produces no smell when crushed: the central yellow portion of the flower heads remain flat when the seeds are ripening and if split vertically the stem is obviously solid. In contrast scented mayweed **F** produces a pleasant smell of chamomile: the central yellow portion becomes cone-shaped after flowering and if split

vertically appears hollow.

Chamomiles resemble mayweeds but if their ripe flower heads are gently rubbed and the florets blown away some flat colourless scales remain: mayweeds have none. Stinking chamomile **A** has a nasty smell and is almost hairless.

A Stinking chamomile *Anthemis cotula*. A hated weed in the days of hand harvesting; leaves and seeds cause painful blisters when rubbed on bare arms. Flowers July—September.

B Oxeye daisy *Leucanthemum vulgare*. Tiny forms occur on cliff-tops and windswept downs; fresh plants boiled made a drink used to cure asthma and ulcers. Flowers June—September.

C Daisy *Bellis perennis*. Rarely produces seed in Britain; spreads in patches in short grass where the prostrate leaves are too low for mechanical or animal mowers to collect. Flowers March—October.

D Feverfew *Tanacetum parthenium*. Leaves have a strong aroma, unpleasant to some people; the name is a corruption of febrifuge — a substance putting fevers to flight. Flowers July—September.

E Pineappleweed *Matricaria matricarioides*. Introduced from South America in 1871, now everywhere in well-trodden places on roadsides, paths and gateways. Flowers June—July.

F Scented mayweed *Matricaria recutita*. Heads less than 3cm across with ray florets which soon turn down **Fa**. Flowers June—July.

G Scentless mayweed *Tripleurospermum inodorum*. Heads up to almost 4cm across with ray florets remaining horizontal **Ga**; sea mayweed with heads 4–5cm across is abundant on shingle, cliffs and rocks. Flowers July—September.

A

B

C

D

E

F

Fa

Ga

G

Daisies: many headed

There are several very common members of the daisy family which not only have their 'flowers' made up of many florets, but also these flower heads themselves are so close together that they make one large almost continuous flowering area.

Perhaps the best known is yarrow **A** which grows up to 50cm tall in grassland everywhere. Its flat rafts of flowers may be white, pink or, rarely, deep purple and make a conspicuous show especially on roadsides in midsummer. Formerly much prized as a wound herb and called *Achillea* because Achilles is said to have used it to heal his soldiers' injuries.

The commonest now in towns and gardens is Canadian fleabane **C** where it grows at the bottom of walls, in cracks in the pavements and on builders' rubble. It arrived in London from North America on board ship about 1690 and is still spreading.

Mugwort **B** is another roadside and rubble species. It is an unlovely plant with dusty, divided leaves and dirty-brown flowers **Ba** as if sprayed with muck by passing cars.

Tansy **F** also grows in rubble, on railway banks and in other waste places near gardens from which it doubtless escaped. Distinctive and distinguished by its branched almost flat inflorescence of golden-yellow button-like heads and finely divided leaves.

The last two plants with clustered heads grow in wet places and have reddish flowers. Butterbur **E** produces spikes of flowers on stream banks in early spring followed by enormous rhubarb-like leaves in May. These were used for wrapping butter and are large enough to make a sunshade.

Hemp-agrimony **D** is related neither to agrimony nor to hemp though the opposite, downy leaves resemble those of hemp. It may line the bank of a small stream or festoon a sea cliff in summer: almost confined to coastal Scotland.

A Yarrow *Achillea millefolium*. Once called 'nose-bleed' because the leaves 'being put in the nose caused it to bleed'. It would certainly irritate because the leaves are finely divided into feather-like segments. Flowers June—September.

B Mugwort *Artemisia vulgaris*. A hazard for hay-fever sufferers: fine pollen is carried in the wind; better stay at home than take advantage of its magical powers of keeping away the forces of darkness.

C Canadian fleabane *Erigeron canadensis*. Leaves long and narrow; greenish-white flowers grouped in a cone-shaped cluster of individual heads less than 6mm across. Flowers August—September.

D Hemp-agrimony *Eupatorium cannabinum*. One of few daisies with opposite leaves; called 'raspberries and cream' in Dorset because clusters sometimes contain a mixture of reddish and white heads. Flowers July—September.

E Butterbur *Petasites hybridus*. Plants may be male or female: over most of British Isles only male spikes occur; the female spikes grow larger and are confined to the middle and north of England. Flowers March—May.

F Tansy *Tanacetum vulgare*. All parts of plant have a strong, spicy scent and an exceedingly bitter taste, nevertheless valued as a flavouring for cakes, puddings and omelettes. Flowers July—September.

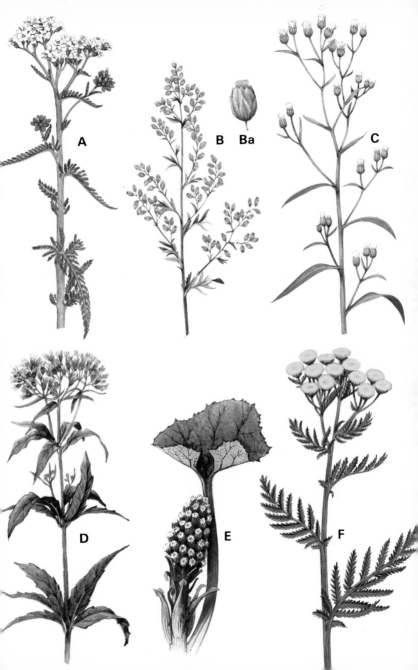

Yellow spikes

Though only two of the plants on this page are in the same family they have in common tall relatively unbranched stems up to half a metre or more high terminating in a spike of stalkless or shortly stalked yellow flowers: at least three should be recognised.

The tallest is great mullein **F** a biennial which produces a dense spike of 5-petalled flowers on stiff stems up to almost 2m tall, hence its other name 'Aaron's-rod' which 'was budded, and brought forth buds and bloomed blossoms'. The whole plant is covered in thick woolly hairs making even their leaves recognisable in winter.

The showiest yellow spikes in gardens are goldenrods. Those normally cultivated were introduced from North America and have escaped to become established on railway banks and other waste places. Our goldenrod **E** is a modest plant less than a metre tall, but individual flower heads are attractive with conspicuous ray florets like ragwort.

Common evening-primrose **B** is another biennial which was also introduced from North America as a garden plant. It has escaped and become widely naturalised in sand dunes, on railway banks and builders' plots: The fragrant flowers open early on summer evenings when they are visited by night-flying moths.

The commonest yellow-spike on roadsides is agrimony **A**: most easily recognised in fruit when the hardened calyx develops a ring of hooked bristles **Aa** which become easily attached to clothes and fur. The leaves are aromatic and were formerly used in herb teas to protect the voices of actors and singers.

The last two yellow spikes belong to the same family, the Resedaceae, which is centred on the Mediterranean. They have irregular flowers with deeply lobed petals of different sizes, the largest at the top. Both are found on roadsides and disturbed places like quarries, especially on chalk or limestone soils. Weld **D** has simple undivided leaves and 4 sepals and petals **Da** whereas wild mignonette **C** has lobed or divided leaves and sepals and petals in sixes.

See also common toadflax, melitot, St. John's-wort, wintercress, yellow archangel, yellow rattle.

A Agrimony *Agrimonia eupatoria*. A member of the rose family, each flower stays open for 3 days; if not pollinated by insects the anthers bend towards the stigma and self-pollination occurs. Flowers June—August.

B Common evening-primrose *Oenothera biennis*. Not a true primrose but a member of the willowherb family with flowers producing 4 valved pods splitting from the top, but the seeds lack plumes. Flowers June—September.

C Wild mignonette *Reseda lutea*. Greenish-yellow flowers develop into 3-chambered pods; mignonette is from the French meaning 'little darling', originally applied to a fragrant garden species *Reseda odorata*. Flowers June—August.

D Weld *Reseda luteola*. Known also as 'dyers' weed'; one of the oldest and best dye plants producing a brilliant and fast yellow used in medieval times for cotton and wool. Flowers June—August.

E Goldenrod *Solidago virgaurea*. Formerly called 'wound weed', *solidago* means 'I consolidate' (wounds); flower spikes are most attractive to butterflies and wasps. Flowers July—September.

F Great mullein *Verbascum thapsus*. Closely related to foxglove and with similar rosette of leaves and tall flowering stem, but with regular 5-petalled flowers with 5, often hairy, stamens. Flowers June—August.

Orchids

Orchids are often thought of as exotic, tropical plants, but over 50 different kinds grow wild in Britain, many producing spikes of colourful and attractive flowers. Each flower consists of 3 sepals and 3 petals alternating with them. Two of the petals are similar to the sepals but the third, the lip or labellum, is developed into various shapes, e.g. pouch, tongue, or mimicking insects such as bees or flies.

The easiest place to find orchids is in deciduous woodland where a sequence of species is in flower from early spring until late summer. First is early-purple orchid **F** recognised even before it flowers by rosettes of blunt, glossy, round-spotted leaves on the forest floor: in April come the spikes of purplish-crimson flowers, the 'long-purples' which surrounded the drowned Ophelia.

This is followed in mid-May by common spotted-orchid **B**. The leaves are marked with transversely elongated dark blotches; the pink flowers are covered in a network of leaves and the middle lobe of the lip is longer than the lobes on either side. Heath spotted-orchid **A** is similar but, as the name suggests, grows on heaths and·other particularly wet, acid soils — rarely in woods. The middle lobe of the lip is always much smaller than the 2 side lobes; the petals are marked with dots and short lines.

The third common woodland orchid to flower (in June) is probably common twayblade **D**, easy to recognise by its conspicuous 'tway blades' — the pair of round, almost opposite, leaves at the base. The flowers are not so conspicuous but have a fascinating man-like appearance **Da**.

The last woodland orchid of summer continuing into autumn is broad-leaved helleborine **C**. The basal leaves are broad not unlike twayblade but are never opposite; the upper ones are narrower; the dingy somewhat one-sided spikes may have as many as 100 flowers.

The most exciting common orchid is the bee orchid **E** because it is both beautiful and unpredictable: rarely found with certainty in the same place each year, its numbers vary wildly from a few to thousands. Most frequent in recently disturbed lime-rich soils.

A Heath spotted-orchid, *Dactylorhiza maculata*. All leaves narrow and acute, lightly marked with almost circular spots, only 1–3 on stem, rest at base. Never in woods, abundant in north and west Britain. Flowers June—August.

B Common spotted-orchid *Dactylorhiza fuchsii*. Lowest leaf broadly elliptic and blunt-pointed; most are heavily marked with transverse spots, 3–5 leaves on stem. Abundant in woods, marshes, downs and dunes with some lime in soil. Flowers June—August.

C Broad-leaved helleborine *Epipactis helleborine*. Variable in height and number of flowers; ribbed leaves, spiral round stem; the dingy greeny-brown flowers are drooping and turned to one side. Flowers July—October.

D Common twayblade *Listera ovata*. Flies and beetles trigger an explosive mechanism which attaches pollen sacks to their head or back so they pollinate the next flower they visit. Flowers June—July.

E Bee orchid *Ophrys apifera*. Lip marked to resemble the velvety body of a female bumblebee; however visits by male bees are rare, most are self-fertilised in Britain. Flowers June—July.

F Early-purple orchid *Orchis mascula*. Common names like 'Priest's pintel' and 'cock-flower' refer to the two root tubers which resemble a pair of testicles. Flowers April—June.

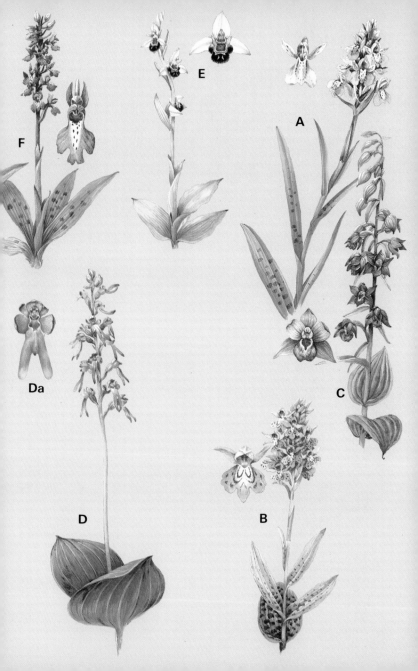

Grasses 1

Superficially it may seem that all grasses look alike, but with very little effort it is easy to recognise and name the common ones.

Leave a small area of your lawn uncut for study at hay-time. You will soon see 3 main types of grass flowering heads and cock's-foot (p. 114, **D**) is unique. At ground level its large greyish-green leaves are folded from a strong keel with a prominent white flange — a ligule — where leaf joins stem.

The three main types are (i) the spike with separate spikelets (groups of flowers) attached to a single main stalk, e.g. perennial rye-grass (p. 114, **H**); (ii) the cylinder in which all the spikelets overlap so that the main stalk is not visible (at least from one side), e.g. meadow foxtail (p. 114, **A**); (iii) the bush in which the inflorescence is much branched with spikelets on fine branches waving in the wind, e.g. all the grasses on this page.

Annual meadow-grass **G** is the common grass you weed from your path: it has bright green leaves with transverse crinkling. Smooth meadow-grass **H** and rough meadow grass **I** are perennials with inflorescences similar to annual meadow grass. The first is upright, shaped like a Christmas tree on a stem smooth when rubbed *gently*; the second curves at the top and has a rough stem.

Creeping bent **A** forms greyish-green circular patches on lawns and has a more feathery inflorescence than the meadow grasses. The best lawns are composed of red fescue **E** in which the fine, needle-like leaves form a dense, uniform mat.

Many grasses have spikelets with long protruding hairs (awns). Two are annuals of garden beds and fence lines. Soft-brome **C** is softly hairy with neat, compact, upright spikelets; barren brome **D** has more open drooping spikelets on roughly hairy stalks.

False oat-grass **B** is the commonest grass of uncut roadsides: up to just over a metre tall and almost silvery.

Common reed **F** is our tallest wild grass reaching over 3m and covering areas of shallow water at the edge of rivers, etc. The 'ligule' is a ring of hairs.

A Creeping bent *Agrostis stolonifera*. Short, sharply pointed leaves with conspicuous sharply pointed ligule. Flowers July—August.

B False oat-grass *Arrhenatherum elatius*. Yellowish, knotted underground stems; leaves at narrow angle to stem. Flowers June—September.

C Soft-brome *Bromus mollis*. Tufted annual, variable in size; spikelets up to 3cm long, variegated green and silver; ligule short. Flowers May—July.

D Barren brome *Bromus sterilis*. Individual spikelets, including awns up to 6cm long made up of 4–10 separate flowers; ligule long-toothed at tip. Flowers May—July.

E Red fescue *Festuca rubra*. Lower leaves fine, needle-like, but flat on flowering stem and ridged on upper surface; stems at ground level dark reddish. Flowers May—June.

F Common reed *Phragmites australis*. Stems and leaves are tough and persistent. Flowers August—October.

G Annual meadow-grass *Poa annua*. Tufted annual with spreading noticeably flattened stems and leaves with hooded apex; ligules long, finely toothed at tip. Flowers all year round.

H Smooth meadow-grass *Poa pratensis*. Creeping species of well-trodden turf; leaves with parallel sides ending abruptly in hooded apex; ligule short and blunt. Flowers May—July.

I Rough meadow-grass *Poa trivialis*. Creeping species of damp grassland, etc.; red at base of stem; leaves narrowing gradually to the point; ligule long and pointed. Flowers June—July.

A B C D E

F G H I

Grasses 2

The only 'bushy-topped' grass on this page is Yorkshire-fog **B**. The whole plant is covered in soft hairs making it appear greyish-green as seen in a fog. The base of the stem hidden in the turf, is decorated with vertical pink stripes.

Apart from cock's-foot **D** the remaining grasses illustrated are either spikes or cylinders. The two commonest grasses with spike-like inflorescences are shown here: both are likely to be found in any garden or nearby grassland. Perennial rye-grass **H** has spikelets which alternate on opposite sides of a zig-zag stalk attached so that when the spike is viewed from the side, as in the illustration, the spikelets are seen from the side also. Common couch **E** has the spikelets similarly arranged but when the spike is viewed from the side the spikelets are seen end on.

Of the five 'cylindrical' grasses the most instantly recognisable is wall barley **G**, a hairy annual in which the flowers develop awns up to 3cm long. A common wallside and 'pavement' grass in towns and villages in the lowlands.

Crested dog's-tail **C** is almost equally distinctive because the 'cylinder' is one-sided with the fine wavey stalk clearly visible if turned. Common in old grassland, often showing in winter because stock avoid the wiry stems.

Sweet vernal-grass **F** has cylinders which are loosely arranged so that the stem may often be seen between the spikelets. Formerly sown in pastures for the fragrant smell it gave to hay, detectable when leaves are rubbed.

Meadow foxtail **A** is the earliest 'cylinder' to flower beginning in April when it can be distinguished from the superficially similar timothy **I** by the silky, purplish sheen and the obvious awns up to 6mm long. As the name suggests meadow foxtail is frequent in old grasslands particularly those which are damp and low-lying in river valleys.

In contrast timothy, one of our most widely sown fodder grasses, is found in a wide range of soils from dry grasslands to lush pastures.

A Meadow foxtail *Alopecurus pratensis*. Hairless leaves all with a short blunt ligule at the base; throughout the lowlands. Flowers April—June.

B Yorkshire-fog *Holcus lanatus*. In meadows, pastures, waste land and open woodland in every corner of the British Isles. Flowers May—August.

C Crested dog's-tail *Cynosurus cristatus*. Hairless leaves with a long fine tip and blunt ligule. Flowers June—August.

D Cock's-foot *Dactylis glomerata*. Broad leaves emerge folded about the middle; one of our commonest fodder grasses sown in pastures everywhere. Flowers June—September.

E Common couch *Elymus repens*. Strong white underground stems spread rapidly in cultivated ground, making it a serious garden and arable weed. Flowers June—August.

F Sweet vernal-grass *Anthoxanthum odoratum*. Leaves loosely covered in hairs, and densely at the base of the long blunt ligule. Flowers May—July.

G Wall barley *Hordeum murinum*. Base of leaf produces narrow projections (auricles) which wrap round the stem and overlap. A favourite with children who put it in sleeves and feel it creep up. Flowers May—August.

H Perennial rye-grass *Lolium perenne*. Shiny green, hairless leaves with a short, blunt ligule and projecting auricles at the base. Flowers May—August.

I Timothy *Phleum pratense*. Hairless leaves with long blunt ligule; base of stem divided into 2—3 short swollen sections. Flowers June—August.

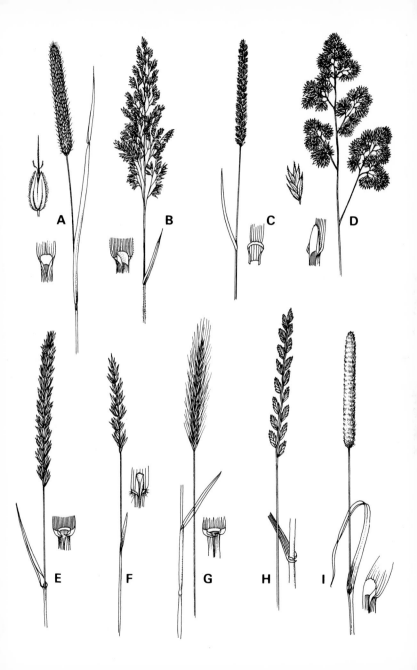

A   B   C   D

E   F   G   H   I

Wetlands and ponds 1

Most gardens are not large enough to have their own marshy area where water covers the surface for much of the winter and the water-table remains high in summer. The nearest substitute which many now contain is a small garden pond with edges which provide some of the features of marshland.

Water-plantain **A** is one of our commonest water plants growing at the shallow edge of rivers, canals, ditches and ponds throughout the lowlands. Recognised by having leaves like greater plantain (page 88) rising from the water and leafless stems up to about a metre tall producing 3-petalled pale-lilac flowers open in the afternoon only. It spreads by corm-like tubers produced from the roots. The roots are edible once their bitter taste has been removed by drying.

The yellow iris or flag **D** is another pond-side plant where its greyish-green flattened leaves occur in large patches. It also grows in wet woods and rushy meadows where it spreads by stout stems similar to those used to propagate garden irises. Each flowering stem produces 2–3 flowers which appear one at a time from spring through summer.

Marsh pennywort **C** is a rushy-meadow plant *par excellence*: its conspicuous circular leaves up to 5cm across are almost certain to be found covering the surface. Finding the flowers is much more difficult: they are tiny, green and hidden beneath the leaves. They are arranged in irregular clusters unlike the neat umbels of the parsley family to which it belongs. However the fruits are unmistakeable and similar to hemlock **Ca**.

Meadowsweet **B** can be seen and smelt from a distance by the drifts of creamy white in wet meadows made up of thousands of its feathery flower heads. It belongs to the rose family and each flower has 5 petals and numerous stamens **Ba** producing a cluster of ripe fruits in the centre which soon become twisted in a spiral. This is the origin of the name *Spiraea*, the well known, closely related, garden plants.

A Water-plantain *Alisma plantago-aquatica*. Each flower produces a whorl of numerous fruits flattened together like the segments of an orange, each with a style arising below the middle **Aa**. Flowers June—August.

B Meadowsweet *Filipendula ulmaria*. Once gathered, dried and strewn on the floors of medieval homes to disguise less pleasant odours; also used to flavour drinks and to sweeten mead; it takes its name from this, rather than from meadows. Flowers June—September.

C Marsh pennywort *Hydrocotyle vulgaris*. Once cursed by farmers as a cause of liver rot in sheep, although the real culprit was the liver-fluke which also flourishes in marshy meadows. Flowers June—August.

D Yellow iris *Iris pseudacorus*. The flattened stems yield a black dye once used in ink-making; coffee-bean sized seeds make a coffee-like drink after roasting. Flowers May—July.

A

Aa

Ba

B

D

Ca

C

Wetlands and ponds 2

Two large-flowered water-lilies grow wild in Britain and both would grace the garden lily-pond. White water-lily **D** with round leaves and flowers as much as 15cm across, is the commoner in the north and west. It is related to the buttercup family, and no flowers show more closely than these the resemblance between petals and stamens as they grade into each other — a characteristic of primitive families. A further interest is the way the petals collapse at night so the flower sinks below the surface, expanding and re-emerging the next morning.

Yellow water-lily **C** has oval leaves and smaller flowers up to 5cm across, and is the commoner in the south and east. Both have massive rhizomes to anchor them to the bottom of the lakes, ponds and slow-moving rivers they inhabit. Leaves and flowers ascend from the bottom and float because their stems are spongy and full of air.

Bogbean **A** grows not only in bogs but also in shallow ponds and round the margins of small lakes where the water is at or above the surface all year round. For most of that year it can only be recognised by the large trifoliate bean-like leaves, up to 10cm across. But it is not a bean (or pea) but is closely related to the gentian family. This can be best appreciated when the handsome pink and white flowers with 5 hairy petals appear in May. Visitors to bogs in summer find only the spikes of spherical capsules.

Purple-loosestrife **B** is a handsome perennial often growing just over a metre in height beside sluggish rivers, canals, lakes and even small ponds where it may form a purplish misty margin from mid-summer until the frosts of autumn. It occurs throughout the lowlands of England but only near the south and west coast of Scotland. A member of a mainly tropical family, Lythraceae related to the willowherbs, of which *Lythrum* is the only genus native to Europe.

A Bogbean *Menyanthes trifoliata.* Plant has a bitter taste and dried leaves were used as a substitute for hops in beer-making in northern England. Flowers May—June.

B Purple-loosestrife *Lythrum salicaria.* Three forms occur with flowers differing in length of stamens and styles; Darwin showed pollination only completely effective when styles receive pollen from stamens of same length. Flowers June—September.

C Yellow water-lily *Nuphar lutea.* Also called 'Brandy-bottle' because the flowers smell of stale brandy and the capsule which develops after the petals fall is shaped like a green-glazed carafe **Ca**. Flowers June—August.

D White water-lily *Nymphaea alba.* The dried rootstock was thought by the ancients to be the source of a cure for dysentry: their descendents dissent. Flowers July—August.

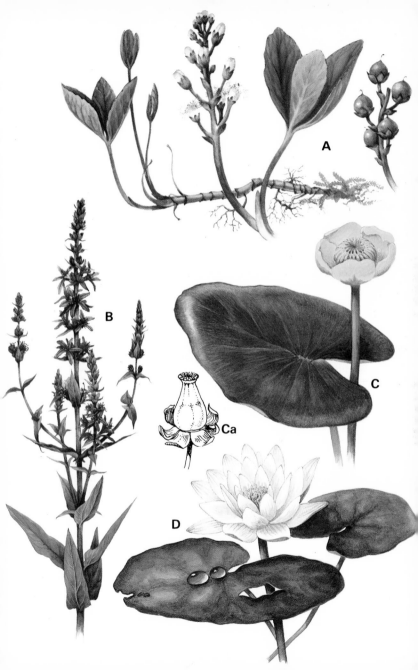

A

B

Ca

C

D

Woodlands and shrubberies

The natural vegetation of Britain below about 600m is broad-leaved woodland. Though over 90% of that woodland has been felled, many of the characteristic plants linger on in hedgerow, copse and spinney and may even be found in shady corners of large old gardens: new houses built in old grounds may have gardens with similar treasures.

Bluebell **C** is one of the wonders of the woods in spring, especially to the foreign visitor because it only grows on the western edge of Europe and only in such masses in the British Isles. Bluebells in most gardens are the bigger Spanish species in which the flowering stem is erect, not drooping, and the anthers blue, not cream.

Lords-and-ladies **A** is one of our most familiar yet strange wildflowers, recognisable from the moment the arrow-shaped leaves appear in hedge banks with the first warmth of spring. In April a pale-green sheath edged with purple (the spathe) appears which encloses a long fleshy rod (the spadix) with separate male and female flowers hidden below. Pollination is carried out by small flies attracted by a manure-like smell and trapped until the spathe withers.

Wood-sorrel **E** has unmistakeable clover-like leaves and shares with clover an ability to fold down the three segments. However in wood-sorrel this takes place not only at night but in response to strong sunlight. The regular 5-petalled solitary flowers are distinctly un-clover like. Extremely tolerant of shade it can grow in the darkest beech-woods.

Enchanters'-nightshade **B** also grows in dark and shady woods. This dull relative of the willowherbs can be a troublesome plant. It produces little egg-shaped fruits **Ba** with trouser-gripping bristles to carry it to your shrubbery where its long creeping underground roots make it a difficult weed to eradicate.

Wood avens **D**, a member of the rose family, also has fruits with hooked bristles which easily catch on clothing and fur. However the bright, upright, yellow flowers, though small, make it a just acceptable garden visitor. Water avens (not illustrated) with large, nodding, orange-pink flowers would be even more welcome in a damp corner where it could rival the cultivated geums.

A Lords-and-ladies *Arum maculatum*. Red berries which appear in July and August are poisonous; forms with spotted leaves are commonest in southern England. Flowers April—May.

B Enchanter's-nightshade *Circaea lutetiana*. Circe was an enchantress who turned the crew of Ulysses into pigs; small flowers have only 2, deeply notched, petals and 2 stamens. Flowers June—August.

C Bluebell *Hyacinthoides non-scripta*. Stems arise from a small bulb 15cm below the ground which contains a slimy juice once used as a glue for arrows. Flowers April—June.

D Wood avens *Geum urbanum*. The root has a clove-like smell and was used as an additive to flavour ale and chewed as an antidote to bad breath. Flowers June—August.

E Wood-sorrel *Oxalis acetosella*. Forms patches spreading by slender creeping underground stems; flower stalks longer than leaf stalks with 2 tiny scales in the middle. Flowers April—May.

Ba

A

B

C

D

E

Glossary

Words in *italic* indicate a cross reference to another entry in the glossary.

achene a small, dry, single-seeded fruit, e.g. burdock, dandelion, thistle

annual a plant which produces flowers and seeds and dies within a year, e.g. shepherd's-purse

anther the top part of the *stamen*, containing pollen

auricles small projections, often overlapping, at base of a leaf, e.g. rye-grass

awn a bristle-like projection from the flowers of grasses, e.g. sterile brome, or from the tips of leaves

berry a fleshy fruit often containing several seeds, e.g. bittersweet

biennial a plant which flowers and seeds and then dies in its second year, e.g. wild carrot

bract the reduced, leaf-like part of a plant beneath the flower stalk on which one or many flowers grow, e.g. yellow rattle.

bulb an underground organ made up of swollen fleshy leaves enclosing next year's bud

calyx the *sepals* of a flower, joined or separate

capsule a dry fruit consisting of 2 or more seed-containing compartments, round or quadrangular in cross section, e.g. poppy

corm a short, round, swollen (usually vertical) underground stem with next year's bud on the top

corolla the *petals* of a flower, joined or separate

deciduous plants which lose their leaves in autumn, e.g. bilberry

dioecious having separate male and female plants, e.g. dog's mercury

exserted the projecting of *anthers* beyond the surrounding flower parts, e.g. water mint

florets reduced flowers making up the heads characteristic of the daisy family

fruit seed or seeds and the structure surrounding them, which may be fleshy or dry, e.g. blackberry or shepherd's-purse.

glabrous hairless

gland a small, globular object, often on a short stalk, containing sticky or aromatic substances, e.g. sticky groundsel

hermaphrodite having flowers with both male and female organs, i.e. *stamen* and *ovary*

hybrid a plant resulting from the fertilisation of one species by pollen from another species

labellum the lip of a flower, often large and showy; in orchids the lower of 3 petals, e.g. bee orchid

latex a milky juice, e.g. sow-thistle

leaflet the leaf-like subdivisions of a leaf lacking any *stipules* at the base, e.g. clovers

ligule a small, often colourless, flange of tissue at the point where a leaf joins the stem of a grass, e.g. cock's-foot

linear a long, narrow, parallel-sided leaf

mucro the short narrow point of a leaf, leaflet, capsule, etc., e.g. black medick leaflet

nectar a sugary substance exuded from nectaries at the base of *petals*

node a position on a stem where one or more leaf stalks join it

opposite pairs of leaves or flowers at the same level on opposite sides of a stem

ovary an organ consisting of 1 or more compartments containing the developing seeds (ovules)

perennial a plant which lives for more than 2 years and usually produces flowers and seeds each year.

perianth the *sepals* and *petals* of a flower together; often used when sepals and petals are indistinguishable, e.g. marsh-marigold

petal a segment of the inner *whorl* of the leaf-like parts of a flower, usually brightly coloured

pod a dry fruit usually consisting of 1–2 seed compartments flattened in cross section, e.g. common vetch

pollen the minute product of the *anthers*, containing male 'sperm' which fertilise the ovules to form seeds

pollination process of transmitting pollen from anthers to stigmas so that fertilisation may occur. Effected by animals, especially insects, wind, water or, within the same flower, by self-pollination

raceme a conical-shaped flowering stem with the youngest and smallest branches or flowers at the top

ray floret *florets* at the margin of the 'flower' of a member of the daisy family in which the *corolla* is either expanded on one side to produce a 'petal', or simply larger and more conspicuous than the inner florets

reflexed bent abruptly at more than a right angle

rhizome a *perennial*, underground stem, e.g. yellow iris

rosette a ring of leaves at the base of a stem, pressed flat to the soil, e.g. greater plantain

sepal a segment of the outer *whorl* of the leaf-like parts of a flower, usually green

septum a partition between the segments of a fruit, e.g. scurvy grass

spike a simple *raceme* with all flowers on very short stalks, e.g. agrimony

spikelet a collection of *florets* in grasses, usually with 2 *bracts* (glumes) at the base

spur a hollow, often cone-shaped, projection from the base of a *petal* or *corolla*, e.g. violets

stamen the male reproductive organ of a plant, consisting of a filament with an *anther* at the top

stigma the portion of the female part of the flower at the top of the *style* which receives the *pollen*

stipuie a leaf-like appendage at the base of a leaf stalk where it joins the stem and sometimes attached to it, e.g. clovers

style the portion of the female part of the flower bearing the *stigma* at the top

tendril a part of a leaf or stem modified to act as a climbing organ, e.g. vetches

tooth a serration at the edge of a leaf

tuber a swollen part of a stem or root which lasts for less than a year and does not produce another attached to it, e.g. bulbous buttercup

umbel an umbrella-shaped arrangement of flowers in which all the flower stalks arise from the top of the stem, e.g. all members of the carrot family

whorl 3 or more organs of the same kind arising at the same level on a stem, e.g. leaves of bedstraws

---

The Royal Society for Nature Conservation
The Green, Nettleham, Lincoln, LN2 2NR

The Royal Society for Nature Conservation is the national association of the 46 local Nature Conservation Trusts which forms the major voluntary organisation concerned with all aspects of wildlife conservation in the United Kingdom. The Trusts have a combined membership of 155,000 and, together with the Society, own or manage 1,500 nature reserves throughout the UK covering a range of sites, from woodland and heathland to wetland and estuarine habitats. Most Trusts have full-time staff but the members themselves, with a wide range of skills, contribute greatly to all aspects of the work.

WATCH: The Watch Trust for Environmental Education
Junior section of the RSNC. Provides exciting environmental projects and local activities for all young people up to 18.

If you would like details of your local Nature Conservation Trust or its junior branch, WATCH, write to RSNC headquarters.

Further reading

Briggs, M., *The Guinness Book of Wild Flowers*. Guinness Superlatives, London, 1980.

Clapham, A. R., Tutin, T. G. & Warburg, E. F., *Excursion Flora of the British Isles* (3rd ed.). Cambridge University Press, Cambridge, 1981.

Fitter, R. S. R., Fitter, A. & Blamey, M., *Wild Flowers of Britain and Northern Europe*. Collins, London, 1974.

Launert, Edmund, *The Country Life Guide to Edible and Medicinal Plants*. Country Life, 1981.

McClintock, D. & Fitter, R. S. R., *Pocket Guide to Wild Flowers*. Collins, London, 1956.

Martin, W. Keble, *Concise British Flora in Colour*. Ebury Press, London, 1965.

Rose, F., *Wild Flower Key to the British Isles and North-West Europe*. Frederick Warne, London, 1981.

Index

127